Mid-Century Vegas

1930s to 1960s

Donald D. Spencer

Schiffer Publishing Ltd

4880 Lower Valley Road Atglen, Pennsylvania 19310

Dedication

To my son Steven,
A fellow casino chip collector.

Other Schiffer Books by Donald D. Spencer

Greetings from St. Augustine, 978-0-7643-2802-2, $24.95
Greetings from Tampa, 978-0-7643-2898-5, $24.95
Greetings from Ormond Beach, 978-0-7643-2809-1, $24.95
Greetings from Daytona Beach, 978-0-7643-2806-0, $24.95

Other Schiffer Books on Related Subjects

Los Angeles Neon, 0-7643-1542-0, $29.95
More Hollywood Homes, 978-0-7643-2902-9, $14.95
Scare-Izona, A Travel Guide to Arizona's Spookiest Spots, 978-0-7643-2844-2, $14.95
Ghosts of Portland, Oregon, 978-0-7643-2798-8, $12.95
Greetings from Portland, Oregon, 0-7643-2576-0, $24.95

Covers by: Bruce Waters
Type set in Souvenir Lt.
ISBN: 978-0-7643-3129-9
Printed in China

Photo Credits

Donald Spencer's postcard, photograph, and memorabilia collections form the base for this book, augmented by b/w photographs from the University of Nevada at Las Vegas (pages 8, 10, 14, 15, 16, 26, 28, 34, & 83) & the Las Vegas News Bureau (pages 53, 72, 84, 100, 101, 131, 133, 134, 148, & 149).

Schiffer Books are available at special discounts for bulk purchases for sales promotions or premiums. Special editions, including personalized covers, corporate imprints, and excerpts can be created in large quantities for special needs. For more information contact the publisher:

Published by Schiffer Publishing Ltd.
4880 Lower Valley Road
Atglen, PA 19310
Phone: (610) 593-1777; Fax: (610) 593-2002
E-mail: Info@schifferbooks.com

For the largest selection of fine reference books on this and related subjects, please visit our web site at:
www.schifferbooks.com
We are always looking for people to write books on new and related subjects. If you have an idea for a book please contact us at the above address.

This book may be purchased from the publisher.
Include $5.00 for shipping.
Please try your bookstore first.
You may write for a free catalog.

In Europe, Schiffer books are distributed by
Bushwood Books
6 Marksbury Ave.
Kew Gardens
Surrey TW9 4JF England
Phone: 44 (0) 20 8392-8585; Fax: 44 (0) 20 8392-9876
E-mail: info@bushwoodbooks.co.uk
Website: www.bushwoodbooks.co.uk
Free postage in the U.K., Europe; air mail at cost.

Contents

Highway Greeting Sign   Photo by Mac Miller

Preface

It was 1954, seven years after mobster Benjamin "Bugsy" Siegel was liquidated for his crime-related activities while building the Flamingo Hotel and Casino, that I drove from San Diego to Las Vegas in my non-air-conditioned 1953 Pontiac convertible for the first time. The temperature was about 112 degrees. To say the least, I was **HOT**. And then it really got hot. But the call of the golden pot and fabulous Las Vegas lured me on. As I drove up the Las Vegas Strip, I noticed that Kathryn Grayson was starring at the Sahara Hotel, Tallulah Bankhead was appearing with a young singer by the name of Merv Griffin at the Sands Hotel, Freddie Martin and his Orchestra was at the Flamingo Hotel, and at the Last Frontier Hotel, there on the marquee was the name "Ronald Reagan," along with the Continentals, a well-known quartet.

At that time there were seven hotel-casinos on the Strip—El Rancho Vegas, Last Frontier, Flamingo, Thunderbird, Desert Inn, Sahara, Sands; the Silver Slipper Casino on the Strip, and a few downtown casinos that included Golden Nugget, Horseshoe Club, Monte Carlo Club, El Cortez, California Club, Las Vegas Club, and Pioneer Club. My favorite places were the Flamingo, El Rancho Vegas, and Golden Nugget. That's when the corporations weren't there. That's when the other folks were in—the mob guys. I never knew it, but that's what they were. I had just been discharged from the U.S. Marine Corps and was starting college at San Diego State. I have visited Las Vegas several times each year since then and saw the city grow from a small desert town to the adult entertainment capital of the world.

I especially remember the 1950s and 1960s visits, the Golden Years of Vegas, when the casinos had terrific entertainment. You could go to a lounge and see better acts than in the showroom. Major stars were in the lounges, or they would come in and sit in with the acts after the main showroom closed. Sometimes Frank Sinatra would get up on the lounge stage at the Sands while Don Rickles was performing. I still laugh when I think of some of the funny burlesque acts I saw at the Silver Slipper Gambling Hall. This was my very favorite casino for entertainment. It was also the place that started the 69-cent breakfast, which was extremely popular for many years. The jaded visitor could also sample the Sands Hotel's all-night buffet—all you could eat for $1.50.

During the slow time in Las Vegas, December to February, many of the casino showrooms had only a few dozen people sitting in the audience. And the shows were free or cost only a few dollars. The lounge shows were always free. In 1954 proverbial cannonballs could be fired through some of the showrooms. Comedian Jack E. Leonard made a crack to a meager batch of ringsiders at El Rancho Vegas showroom, "Look at this—enough customers to fill a Jaguar."

I remember visiting the Dunes, Riviera, New Frontier, Hacienda, Showboat, Royal Nevada, and Tropicana when they first opened; watching the construction of the Stardust; attending many of the early computer shows at the Las Vegas Convention Center; and getting real-life lessons in playing baccarat, craps, and roulette in the casinos. In 1968 I wrote the book *Game Playing With Computers*, the first book that described how to simulate playing games, including blackjack, slot machines, roulette, and craps, with computers. In 1974 I wrote another book, *Game Playing With BASIC*, which showed early users of microcomputers how to program these computers to play games. Throughout the next twenty years, I used casino games as examples in over two dozen of my computer programming textbooks. In addition to providing many real-life experiences, my early years of Las Vegas gaming also provided many wonderful writing ideas.

Collecting casino memorabilia was another early interest. Over the years I managed to put together a sizeable collection of gaming chips, dice, slot machines, playing cards, gaming books, gaming guides, ashtrays, photographs, postcards, entertainment programs, menus, napkins, swizzle sticks, slot machine coin buckets, matchbooks, and other items. I have taken photographs of almost all of the Las Vegas casinos from the Golden Nugget Gambling Hall to the Wynn Las Vegas. Many of these items are used to illustrate this book.

I personally own about fifty-five years worth of great Las Vegas memories. I hope you enjoy reading about the trip back to the Golden Years of Las Vegas as much as I enjoyed writing about it. — *Donald D. Spencer*

About the Postcard

Early Postcards

Postcards first appeared in Austria in 1869, and in England and France in 1870. These early European cards carried no images; only space on one side for an address, the reverse side was for a message. But they enjoyed an advantage over first-class letter mail; they could be mailed at a reduced rate of postage. The first picture postcards appeared in Germany in 1870. The United States began to issue picture postcards in 1873 in conjunction with the Columbian Exposition in Chicago. These were illustrations on government printed postal cards and on privately printed souvenir cards. On May 19, 1898 private printers were granted permission, by an act of congress, to print and sell cards that bore the inscription "Private Mailing Card." The government granted the use of the word "POST CARD" to private printers December 4, 1901. In this era, private citizens began to take black and white photographs and have them printed on paper with postcard backs. These cards are commonly called Real Photo postcards.

Real Photo Postcards

It was in 1902 that Eastman Kodak marketed its postcard size photographic papers. They quickly followed with a folding camera (model No. 3A) that was specially designed for making Real Photo postcards. To make matters even simpler, an amateur photographer could mail the camera with exposed film to Eastman Kodak. They would develop and print the postcards and return them to the sender with a reloaded camera. These innovations in photography as applied to the postcard captured the public's imagination. It had become possible for anyone who owned a camera to make personalized photo postcards.

Postcards Become Popular

The picture postcard did not come into common use in the United States until after 1900. It was about 1902 that the postcard craze hit the country and it was not long before a wide variety of printed postcards were available: advertising, expositions, political, greetings, and more. Collectors would send postcards to total strangers in faraway places, asking for local cards in return. Some collectors specialized in railroad depots, street scenes, cemeteries, churches, courthouses, farms, holidays, animals, military scenes, casinos, ethnic images, sports, hotels, transportation devices, parks, bathing beauties, industrial scenes, beach scenes, plants, lighthouses, restaurants, space, amusement parks, rivers, Steamboats, and even comic cards; others collected anything they could find. Postcard albums, bought by the millions, were filled with every sort of postcard ever issued. The craze was actually worldwide since many countries had postcards. Acceptance by the public was immediate and enthusiastic. Postcards afforded an easy means of communication. They were an early version of today's email, though slower, of course, relying as they did on mail service.

Divided Back Postcards

Before March 1, 1907, it was illegal to write any message on the same side of the card as the address. For that reason the early postcards often have handwriting all over the sides of the picture and sometimes right across it. Many an otherwise beautiful card was defaced in this way. When postcards first started to go through the mails, they were postmarked at the receiving post office as well as that of the sender, making it easy to see the time involved between post offices—sometimes remarkably brief! The volume of postcards was an important reason for discontinuing the unnecessary second marking around 1910. For years postcards cost only a nickel for six and the postage was a penny, right up to World War II.

The most popular American postcards up to World War I were those made in Germany from photographs supplied by American publishers. At the time of the postcard craze, of course, color photography was still something of a rarity and not commercially viable. For the color cards, black and white photos were touched up, hand-colored, and then generally reproduced by lithography. Lithography consists of transferring the image to a lithographic stone, offset to a rubber blanket, and then printed onto paper. The details in the German produced cards were extremely sharp, and the best of them technically have never been matched since.

The German postcard industry folded up in the summer of 1914, when the war struck Europe, and never revived. Postcards produced during the years 1907 and 1915 had a divided back: the address was to be written on the right side; the left side was for writing messages. Millions of postcards were published during these years. Postcard collectors have hailed these opening years of the twentieth century as the "Golden Age" of postcards. During the golden era of the picture postcard, billions of postcards rolled off the printing presses. In 1917 the United States entered World War I and the postcard craze ended.

White Border Postcards

With the advent of World War I, the supply of postcards for American consumption switched from Germany to England and the United States. Postcards printed in the United States from 1915 to 1930 were classified as White Border cards. To save ink, a colorless border was left around the view. These postcards were of a poorer quality compared to the cards printed in Germany.

Linen Postcards

In 1930 the "linen" textured card was introduced and was popular until 1950. While this card was less expensive to produce, it reduced the clarity of detail in the pictures. These cheap cards are typically printed in vivid colors on paper with a crosshatched surface that resembled linen fabric. "Linen" refers to the texture-like feel of the cardboard stock. The cards of this period romanticized the images of diners, gas stations, hotels, commercial buildings, and tourist attractions. Using the photographic image of an establishment, all undesirable features, such as background clutter, people, telephone poles, and even cars were removed by airbrushing. World War II occupied most people's attention during much of this period, but the prosperity that followed was soon reflected in cards from communities all over the United States. Most of the postcards in this book are linen postcards.

Photochrome Postcards

In 1950 the "photochrome" or "chrome" postcard – those with a glossy finish – replaced the linen card. This type of finish allowed for a very sharp reproduction of the picture, however, the cards seem to have lost much of both the role and nature of earlier cards. The chrome card, which is offered for sale today in gift shops, is where full-color photographic images are reproduced as a half-tone on modern lithography presses. A varnish or lamination is applied on the card to give it a shiny look. In 1970, a king-sized chrome card (4.125" x 5.875") was introduced and by 1978 it was in general use everywhere. This card is also called a continental or modern postcard.

Collecting Postcards

If you have ever browsed through boxes of vintage postcards in an antique shop or at a flea market booth for quaint views of your hometown, you may well be on the way to becoming a deltiologist, which is the collecting and study of postcards. The word deltiology comes from "delti" (little picture) and "logy" (the theory, science, or study of).

Postcards are a compact collectible with a history. They are snapshots in time. In a time when the main communication was by letter, which meant the long process of writing it, the postcard was a quick and simple means of saying "hello" with a picture "worth-a-thousand-words." The postcard's popularity was evidenced when in 1908 the U.S. Post Office cited there were over 677 million postcards mailed, yet the U.S. population was only about 89 million—and this doesn't include those kept as souvenirs. Today, postcard collecting has become the number one hobby in the United States.

Introduction

Welcome to Las Vegas ... undeniably the most exciting city in the world. No other place is as vibrant and alive. It is the most incredible oasis the world has ever known.

Las Vegas shimmers like a dream in the middle of the Mojave Desert. It is a place where reality and fantasy mix, a darkly magical destination that exists as much in the mind as in fact. For its millions of annual visitors, a few days in Las Vegas is a trip to a carnival of earthly delights. It is a place in which time indeed is relative.

Like a dream that unfolds in phases, Las Vegas is many places in one. It's that action-filled adult palace filled with gambling, late-night entertainment, and the intoxicating scent of vice. Over the years, and through infinite changes in fact and fashion, Las Vegas has managed to maintain its magical appeal.

This book is about images, and Las Vegas is where images have been made an art form. The glitter, the lights, the name entertainment, the gambling, and the larger-than-life quality found in Las Vegas are all aspects of that image. It's a visual tour of the most important decades in the history of this magical city. Forget today's gigantic mega-resorts and their huge casinos for just a moment and look back to the formative years, when the hotels were much smaller, when all the popular Hollywood stars entertained in Vegas, when you could have a fine dinner and entertainment and pay for it with pocket change, and when people enjoyed participating in a fantasy vacation. This is the Las Vegas of Yesteryears-Fantastic Vegas in the mid-1900s.

Gambling Pays. Las Vegas is the only large city in the world whose primary industry is entertainment. It has more casinos and more nightlife than any other place on the planet. The entertainment scene has changed considerably through the years and it certainly has become more expensive. These days you can't catch a show like the "Summit" of Frank Sinatra, Dean Martin, Joey Bishop, Peter Lawford, and Sammy Davis, Jr., for $5.95 including dinner. The entertainment and food through the 1940s-1960s was certainly a bargain. Circa 1940s, $5-7.

"Only in Las Vegas." No one can dispute Las Vegas' title as "Entertainment Capital of the World." Wayne Newton once said, "Where else in the world could I have worked for Howard Hughes and his chain of hotels, Desert Inn, Sands, and Frontier for more than 36 weeks a year for 13 years; own my own hotel; and be able to go home and sleep in my own bed each night?" Entertainment guide cover. Circa 1960s, $3-5.

Broadway of the Desert. In the 1950s, the Las Vegas Chamber of Commerce advertised Las Vegas as the "Broadway of the Desert." Nowhere in the world could you find such fun and excitement. One could relax under the friendly Nevada sky during the day and visit the fascinating casinos at night. The clock never stopped and the doors never closed in this resort haven whose welcome was "Howdy Podner, come as you are." Postcard folder cover. Circa 1940s, $7-9.

Welcome to Las Vegas. This welcome sign, one of the most recognizable symbols of Las Vegas, was designed by Betty Willis, a commercial artist, and created by Western Electric Display in 1959. It's located a mile south of the Hacienda Hotel and Casino (now Mandalay Bay Hotel and Casino). The sign greets visitors entering Las Vegas from the south to the fun spot of the west. The reverse side of this sign states: "Drive Carefully. Come back soon." Most visitors do. Circa 1960s, $4-6.

Chapter One:

The Birth of Las Vegas

Nobody knows for sure when people began living in Las Vegas Valley. Ice Age man lived here over 10,000 years ago. He hunted animals that are now extinct.

Then Indian hunters and farmers began living in southern Nevada. Later, the Paiute Indians came to Las Vegas Valley and they still live there. The Paiutes walked the land gathering seeds from plants and trees to eat. Sometimes small animals like rabbits, lizards, or squirrels were caught for food. The Indians lived in the mountains during the hot summer months to escape the heat. When it began to get cold, they moved onto the desert and camped around the springs in the Las Vegas Valley.

The bubbling springs produced a swift stream of water, which flowed across the valley. A large patch of grass grew on each side of the creek. This natural meadow was about one-half mile wide and about three miles in length. This grassy meadow inspired a Spanish explorer to call the place "Las Vegas" (The Meadows in Spanish).

The Las Vegas oasis, shaded with large cottonwood trees, was an important resting place on the Spanish Trail. John C. Fremont traveled the Spanish Trail and camped in Las Vegas May 3, 1844. The famous explorer, Kit Carson, was a guide for this expedition, and Jim Bridger, the well-known mountain man, was a friend of Fremont and Carson.

At that time this whole area, including Las Vegas, was part of Mexico. The United States obtained the Southwest from Mexico in 1848 and Las Vegas became part of the United States.

The Mormons started to settle here in 1855. They cleared land for farms, dug irrigation ditches, and grew crops. They built an adobe fort for protection. The Mormons started a farm to show the Indians how to grow their own food. The

settlers then opened a lead mine on Mt. Potosi and built a smelter to make lead. The lead was needed for bullets.

The Mormons stayed in Las Vegas for less than two years. Eight years after they left, the Mormon Fort was repaired and was used as headquarters for a very successful ranch for over fifteen years.

The Stewart family took over the ranch, but did not move here until 1882. Mr. Stewart was murdered two years later. His widow and five children ran the ranch alone. Helen J. Stewart was very successful at ranching. She had herds of cattle and horses, produced tons of fruit in the orchard, and grew a variety of crops in the fields.

The railroad wanted to lay tracks through southern Nevada. They purchased the 1,800-acre ranch in 1902 for $55,000. Las Vegas was very important for the railroad. It had plentiful water and timber from nearby mountains. As news spread about the railroad shops and roundhouse to be built, hundreds of people came here to buy land and to find jobs with the railroad. Since there were few houses, the new arrivals lived in tents or camped outdoors. The iron horses of the San Pedro, Los Angeles, and Salt Lake Railroad used Las Vegas as a stopover place and watering hole between Salt Lake City and Los Angeles.

The railroad laid out a township of 1,200 lots in 1905 and announced an auction of the properties. Prospective lot buyers came by the scores, mainly from Southern California. After two days of bidding in the 100-degree-plus heat of May 15 and 16, 1905, the auction netted the railroad $265,000. A city awaited building. Upon many of those lots today sit glittering high-rise hotels and casinos.

The railroad wanted saloons built only in one part of town: Block 16, which was bounded by First and Second Streets

Block 16. Along Block 16 during the daytime, everyone sought refuge in the shade, but the evening coolness late in the summer of 1905 brought out the whiskey drinkers and the girls. Saloons outnumbered all other types of businesses combined. The establishments shown here were on the east side of North First Street between Stewart Street and Ogden Avenue. Circa 1905, $7-9.

and Ogden and Stewart Avenues. Back when Las Vegas was founded, it was a row of shacks and saloons: Red Onion Club, Gem Club, Arizona Club, Nevada Club, the Arcade, and some nameless tents and shacks where whiskey, lager beer, and draft beer were served. The Arizona Club became the favorite bar in Las Vegas. The owner decided to build a new and fancy saloon.

A new Arizona Club was built with concrete blocks made in Las Vegas. The second Arizona Club had a grand opening March 31, 1906. It was one-story and thirty feet wide, with a 75-foot-long, hand-carved mahogany bar. Nickel slot machines were installed and drinks cost 15¢. The Arizona Club was the fanciest place west of the Mississippi River, smack in the middle of Block 16. This area became the town's red-light district, and travelers flocked to its saloons, brothels, and gambling halls.

A Spanish-style train depot was built on the west end of Fremont Street in December 1905. The largest dining room in town was called the Beanery. This railroad restaurant sold meals for 15¢. The First State Bank, a twelve-bed hospital, Overland Hotel, and Hotel Nevada all opened in 1906. A year later, a ninety-horsepower single-cylinder engine, affectionately called "Old Betsy," supplied the power to give Fremont Street its first lights. Las Vegas was starting to grow. The Opera House held a symphony in 1909. In 1910 the official population of Las Vegas was 945. The first permanent school opened in 1911—the same year Las Vegas was also incorporated as a town. Beckley's men's store replaced the Opera House building when it burned in 1912—by 1912 Las Vegas was the most active town in southern Nevada.

The first automobile from Los Angeles arrived in Las Vegas in June 1916. It traveled the newly completed all-year road called the Arrowhead Trail. The part of this road near Las Vegas was known as Fifth Street and later as Highway 91, Las Vegas Boulevard, and the Las Vegas Strip. The first airplane landed in Las Vegas in 1920.

Fremont Street, later known as Glitter Gulch, received its first coat of pavement in 1925; five blocks only, from Main Street to Fifth Street. In 1926, Western Air Express began contract airmail service for Las Vegas, near the future site of Club Bingo and Sahara Hotel and Casino The airplane also carried passengers, transporting forty-one during its first year of operation.

The first golf course, built in 1927, had no grass. The fairways were gravel and the greens were sand. The golf course was located at the site of the Las Vegas Convention Center and the Las Vegas Hilton Hotel and Casino. The first air-conditioned building in Las Vegas opened in 1928. A year later, talking motion pictures were shown here. Las Vegas High School was dedicated in 1930. Some people were very angry. They thought a

school for five hundred students was a waste of money and would never be full. The population of Las Vegas that year was 5,165.

Many people had dreamed of controlling the wild Colorado River. Every few years the river caused great damage by flooding farms and ranches in Southern California. Engineers had been planning a dam for the Colorado River since 1902. They finally decided that the best place for the dam was near Las Vegas.

Everyone talked about all the good things that would happen in Las Vegas when the dam was built. A "Welcome To Las Vegas" arch was erected over Fremont Street to welcome visitors to the city. Thousands of people began arriving to see the dam being built. This started a new age of tourism in Las Vegas. The influence and power of the railroad had ended.

Boulder Dam (now Hoover Dam) and Boulder City were started in 1931. This concrete dam is an engineering marvel, as its 726.4-foot-high wall and 660-foot-thick base can store two years average flow of the Colorado River. It took 5,520 men and over a five year period to build its seventy-story-high wall. A mountain of concrete was poured to build the dam. This was enough concrete to build a two-lane highway from New York to San Francisco, over three thousand miles. Lake Mead started to fill when the dam was finished in 1935. Boulder Dam, less than thirty miles from Las Vegas, brought loads of construction workers and money into the city. The area thrived, despite the fact that the country was starting to slide into a Great Depression.

Gambling anyone? Las Vegas and gambling were interconnected from the moment the first tent saloon opened for business. Games of chance challenged the competitive nature of frontiersmen. Here, inside a local tent and wooden saloon, poker players pose for the photograph while creatures of the desert look as though they would like to order a drink. Circa 1905, $5-7.

The Gem Club. Patrons of the Gem Club play roulette, faro, and craps. These fast action games were popular in Western boomtown casinos where gamblers were continually impatient for speedy results. The Gem Club was located at First Street adjoining the Arizona Club in downtown Las Vegas. Circa 1902, $5-7.

Arizona Club. On March 31, 1906 the Arizona Club moved into these spacious Mission-style quarters with elaborately curved windows of leaded, beveled plate glass and matching front doors of solid oak. Concrete blocks made in downtown Las Vegas were used to build the exterior walls. Around 1907 Al James acquired Arizona Club from its builder James O. McIntosh and added a second story with red-light features. The upstairs was regarded as the "niftiest house of joy on the Pacific Coast." The interior finish was of quartered oak with pink Tennessee marble baseboards. The club's crowning glory was the long mahogany bar with an elaborately designed back-bar of imported French plate glass of optic design. The Arizona Club was the top nightspot west of the Colorado River and east of Death Valley in the early 1900s. It brought unrivaled luxury to the town's entertainment scene. Circa 1906, $7-9.

Arizona Club in 1910. Gambling was outlawed throughout Nevada, but clandestine games of chance continued in Las Vegas. Here, gamblers play roulette at Arizona Club with gold coins. Circa 1910, $5-7.

Interior View. An ornate, thirty-foot-long, $23,000 mahogany bar accented the elegant interior of the Arizona Club. It was Las Vegas' finest and everything was first class. In the early 1940s, the bar, along with the beveled-glass front of the building, was moved to the Last Frontier Hotel's Horn Room. Nickel slot machines were installed and drinks cost 15¢. Even though gambling was made illegal in 1911, bars in Block 16 ignored the law. Block 16 developed such a bad reputation that it was closed down by a court order in 1942. Circa 1912, $7-9.

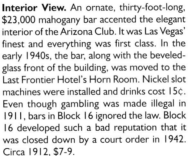

Chapter Two:
The 1930s—
Winds of Change

1930s America

Unemployment and poverty dominated the lives of many people in America at the beginning of the 1930s. Franklin D. Roosevelt was elected President in 1932, offering a "New Deal" for Americans through a wide-ranging recovery program. Dust storms forced many farmers to give up their land. Popular films included "King Kong" and "It Happened One Night." For the first time, African-American athletes became national idols: Joe Louis in boxing and Jesse Owens in track and field. The "Star-Spangled Banner" was chosen as the national anthem. The Empire State Building rose above the Manhattan skyline and the Golden Gate Bridge spanned the San Francisco Bay. The parking meter made its first appearance in 1935. The extreme nationalist and racist Nazi Party came to power in Germany; they imprisoned and killed thousands of Jews while many others were forced to flee their European homeland. The end of the decade saw the onset of World War II.

Looking East on Fremont Street. Las Vegas got its first economic boost in 1931 when construction on Hoover Dam began. While the rest of the nation was experiencing the depression, the Hoover Dam project employed over 5,000 workers. This, along with the passage of a law legalizing gambling and a six-week divorce law, helped Las Vegas fare much better than the rest of the nation during those years. Thousands of people began arriving in Las Vegas to see the dam built. This started a new age of tourism in Las Vegas. The influence and power of the railroad had ended. In this view, Overland Hotel (now Las Vegas Hotel and Casino) is on the left and Hotel Nevada (now Golden Gate Hotel and Casino) is across from it on the right. Circa 1930, $5-7.

1930s Las Vegas

The 1930s began in Las Vegas much like they did throughout the rest of America. The Depression was at its height; Herbert Hoover was in the White House and, because of construction starting on nearby Boulder Dam (later named Hoover Dam), the residents of Las Vegas were certain the city was on its way.

Gambling in Nevada existed in and out of the law since its territorial days, but when the state legislature acted April 28, 1931, all it did was lift a ban that had been imposed sixteen years earlier. That legislation set liberal gambling provisions, and except for modifications setting stringent controls, is still in effect after over seventy-five years of gaming.

Legal gambling got underway in Las Vegas the following month, May 1931, and only six people sought licenses to operate. The first one was issued to a woman, Mayme Stocker, who opened the Northern Club on 15 East Fremont Street. Her husband Harold and the Stocker family were among early settlers engaged in business ventures.

The other five licenses were issued to the Boulder Club, 118 East Fremont Street; Las Vegas Club, 21-23 East Fremont Street; A. T. McCarte's Exchange Club, 123 South First Street; Leo Kind and Thomas Rowan, 127-129 South First Street; and Butter and Marsh, 110 South First Street.

Prior to the era of the Cornero Brothers, who constructed the Meadows, Las Vegas gambling was done in several casinos on or near Fremont Street in the downtown area. The Meadows was built in 1931 by gambler Tony (The Admiral) Cornero and his brothers, Frankie and Louis. The Meadows, located on East Charleston Boulevard outside the city limits, provided Las Vegas with its first real nightclub. It was an elaborate setup. It had a large gambling casino with lookouts conveniently spotted all around the room. These men, all expert riflemen, sat with their trusty Winchesters on their knees, ready to blast any would-be "heister" who might think he could make a killing at the gambling tables without the benefit of playing the games. Across the entry hall was a nightclub that presented the first legitimate floorshow ever seen in Nevada: Judy Garland sang there as one of the "Gumm Sisters."

In 1931 Hotel Nevada (built in 1906 on the southeast corner of Main and Fremont Streets) was enlarged and renamed the Sal Sagev (Las Vegas spelled backwards) Hotel.

12

Meadows Club. During construction of Hoover Dam in the 1930s, Tony Cornero's $100,000 Meadows Club flourished at the far east end of Fremont Street (intersection of Charleston Boulevard and Fremont Street). The operation sported a bank of Mills Poinsettia slot machines, the most popular early jackpot machine of the Mills Novelty Companies line. The machines were attractively adorned with bright red flowers and green leaves. After the dam was completed in 1935, the club closed, but Cornera resurfaced five years later with offshore gambling ships along the southern California coast. He returned to Las Vegas in the mid-1950s and built the Stardust Hotel and Casino. The Meadows was the first nightclub in Las Vegas. Circa 1931, $5-7.

Looking West on Fremont Street. The completion of Hoover Dam gave Las Vegas gambling, legalized in 1931, an impetus toward greater and grander things. These clubs along Fremont Street, a drab section in the 1920s, developed into the casinos and saloons of the 1930s competing for public favor. New clubs also had opened up beside the enlarged, older establishments by the late 1930s. One of the first gambling establishments on Fremont Street was the Boulder Club, shown on the right in this view. The Majestic Theater is shown on the left and the railroad depot, in the far center, at the end of Fremont Street. Circa 1931, $5-7.

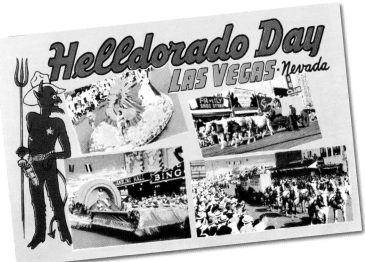

Celebration! An annual spring event, Helldorado Days celebrated the Old West with four days of bustles, hoops, and boisterous fun. Women wore long full skirts, basques, and bonnets of frontier days while men, half lost in beards, wore jeans, boots, colorful shirts, and huge hats. Parades, a rodeo, street dances, and other events intended to re-create the early spirit turned Las Vegas into a rollicking hybrid of two vastly different eras. Circa 1930s, $8-10.

Roulette. A popular game, players crowd a roulette table in a downtown Las Vegas casino. Crowded gaming tables were a common site in this growing western town. Circa 1930s, $8-10.

Bob Russell, a graduate of the University of Southern California law and dental schools, bought the Apache Hotel in 1932 and began some legendary promoting for Las Vegas. The Apache was located on the northwest corner of Second and Fremont Streets. It was the town's first one hundred-room hotel, first three-story structure, and featured the town's first elevator.

A regular at the Apache Hotel was Comedian W. C. Fields, and everyone at the hotel would instantly know when he came to town because the number one priority of the famous comedian was to order two pitchers of martinis and have them sent to his room. The story goes that he once went into the Apache Bar and asked the bartender, "Was I in here last night?" "Yes, you were, Mister Fields," said the bartender. "Did I have a $100-bill with me?" asked Fields. "Yes, you did. You put it on the bar and said, 'Drinks for everybody until this gone.'" "Thank God," exclaimed Fields. "I thought I'd lost it."

Over the years several casinos operated on the first floor of the Apache Hotel: Apache Casino (1934-1941), Western Casino (1941-1944), S. S. Rex Club (1945-1946), Eldorado Club (1947-1951), Binion's Horseshoe (1951-2005), and Binion's (2005-present).

In 1932 J. H. Morgan opened the Nevada Club at 113 East Fremont Street in downtown Las Vegas. Through several owners, the Nevada Club remained at that location until 1969. During the mid-1960s it was known as Diamond Jim's Nevada Club.

Film stars Rex Bell and Clara Bow, Las Vegas' first famous residents, married in a secret ceremony. The star image of the rip-roaring gambling town grew as the Hollywood crowd continued to discover its distinctive offerings.

In 1934 the Boulder Club turned on the town's first neon sign, designed and constructed by the Young Electric Sign Company (YESCO) of Salt Lake City. It was a freestanding, forty-foot sign with vertical letters topping a bright marquee. Four years later the company opened Las Vegas' first full-service sign facility that would create almost seventy-five percent of Las Vegas' neon marvels. By the close of 1946, YESCO had designed and started the race of "Spectaculars" for the Frontier Club, Sal Sagev Hotel, El Rancho Vegas, Pioneer Club, Golden Nugget, the Las Vegas and Eldorado Clubs, and many others!

In 1935 the Elks Club inaugurated a yearly celebration to honor the town's Western heritage; the weeklong fete was called Helldorado Days. It was the town's first major effort to attract visitors and Las Vegas' first convention. Two years later, cowboy star Tex Ritter entertained at the Helldorado celebration, singing "The Rodeo Boys," which he wrote for the occasion.

In 1939 the remodeled Pair-O-Dice Club on Highway 91 (later renamed the Las Vegas Strip) reopened as the Ninety One Club. In 1942 this would become the site of the Last Frontier Hotel.

The following casinos were located in Las Vegas during the 1930s:

Boulder Club, 1931, 118 East Fremont Street
Exchange Club, 1931, 123 South First Street
Frontier Club, 1935, 117 East Fremont Street
Las Vegas Club, 1931, 21-23 East Fremont St.
The Meadows, 1931, East Charleston Blvd.
Nevada Club, 1932, 113 East Fremont Street
Ninety One Club, 1939, Highway 91
Northern Club, 1931, 15 East Fremont Street
Pair-O-Dice Club, 1930, Highway 91
Sal Sagev Casino, 1934, 1 East Fremont Street
Silver Club, 1932, North Second Street.

Apache Casino. A. L. Worswick designed the Apache Hotel in 1931. The Apache was for many years regarded as Las Vegas' plushest hotel. The Apache Casino was on the ground floor along with the Apache Café and Apache Bar. Owned by Las Vegas pioneer P. O. Silvagni, it was possibly the first plush casino in downtown Las Vegas. Among his friends and frequent visitors was dashing movie star, Clark Gable. People spent a lot of time going up and down the building in a modern contraption called an elevator—it was the only one in the whole state! Circa 1930s, $5-7.

Craps. Men at the Apache Casino gather around a craps table with an old fashioned layout. The gamblers were making bets with coins and paper money. Circa 1930s, $7-9.

Fremont Street, Las Vegas, Nevada. This Fremont Street view shows the Boulder Club and Western Casino in the Apache Hotel. By 1947 the Boulder Club had a new neon sign and the Eldorado Club had replaced the Western Casino in the Apache Hotel. The Boulder Club opened in 1929, two years before gambling was legalized in 1931, and was one of the casinos in operation in 1931. The Boulder Club was consumed by fire in 1956. Circa 1945, $14-16.

A Bold Sign. The Boulder Club installed a large, streamlined sign over a marquee angled like a theater's. The sign introduced the fabled Young Electric Sign Company (YESCO) of Salt Lake City, Utah to Las Vegas. Circular blades trimmed the leading edge of this forty-foot sign. Plate glass shaded by Venetian blinds opened the first floor to full view of Fremont Street. A sign also advertised 10¢ craps and the game "21" (blackjack). Circa 1947, $8-10.

Typical Gambling Hall Scene. After gambling was legalized in 1931, the first four Las Vegas gambling clubs were the Boulder, Northern, Las Vegas, and Exchange Clubs. This busy scene was taken in the Boulder Club. It was a typical Fremont Street sawdust joint in a period when a high-ceilinged storefront was crammed with a bar and gaming tables. Circa 1930s, $10-12.

Las Vegas Club. J. Kell Houssels came to Las Vegas as a member of the surveying crew for the Boulder Dam project. When gambling was legalized in 1931, he purchased the Old Smokeshop at the 23 East Fremont Street and turned it into the Las Vegas Club. In 1951 the Las Vegas Club moved to 18 East Fremont Street on the main floor and back of the Overland Hotel. Circa 1934, $7-9.

Gambling Hall. The table games at the Las Vegas Club drew its share of gamblers. Circa 1930s, $7-9.

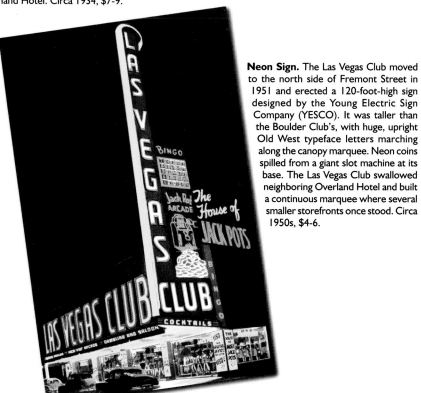

Neon Sign. The Las Vegas Club moved to the north side of Fremont Street in 1951 and erected a 120-foot-high sign designed by the Young Electric Sign Company (YESCO). It was taller than the Boulder Club's, with huge, upright Old West typeface letters marching along the canopy marquee. Neon coins spilled from a giant slot machine at its base. The Las Vegas Club swallowed neighboring Overland Hotel and built a continuous marquee where several smaller storefronts once stood. Circa 1950s, $4-6.

Memorabilia, Las Vegas Club. Playing cards, gaming chips, matchbook, ashtray, and keno form. Circa 1950s-1960s, $1-6.

White Spot Café. Located at 109 East Fremont Street in downtown Las Vegas, White Spot Café was opened in 1932 by J. M. Pappas with a few slot machines. In 1951 the site became the Forty Niner Club and had slot machines, blackjack, poker, and craps tables. A year later, it became the Fortune Club. In 1957 it became the Zodiac Club and in 1959, the Nevada Club, which operated for ten years. In 1969 it became part of the Golden Nugget Gambling Hall. Circa 1930s, $8-10.

Nevada Club. Located at 113 East Fremont Street, the Nevada Club was between the Lucky Strike and California clubs. A free show, "Les Girls de Paris," was performing in the lounge when this photo was taken. Circa 1956, $2-4.

The Attire. Western attire was de rigueur when Las Vegas' motto was "Still a Frontier Town." Here, a big crowd watches a poker game at the Northern Club. When gambling was legalized in 1931, the first gaming license was issued to Mayme V. Stocker for the Northern Club at 15 East Fremont Street in downtown Las Vegas. Circa 1935, $5-7.

Sal Sagev Hotel. The Sal Sagev Hotel opened in the former Hotel Nevada, which was built in 1906. In 1931, the year gambling was legalized in Nevada, the old hotel was enlarged and changed its name to Sal Sagev, which is Las Vegas spelled backwards. The Sal Sagev Casino had roulette, poker tables, and slot machines. In 1955 the casino became the Golden Gate Casino. Circa 1933, $5-7.

Chapter Three:
The 1940s—
The Fabulous Forties

1940s America

The first half of the decade was dominated by a global war in which some fifty-five million people were killed, more of them civilians than military people. After the war, shattered nations slowly pieced themselves together again. America emerged from the war as the world's most popular nation. Americans, after surviving years of depression and World War II, eagerly started families. A surge in the 1946 birthrate began the postwar baby boom. Movie fans enjoyed the films of Betty Grable and Bing Crosby. Commercial television was launched; Milton Berle and Ed Sullivan became household names. Jackie Robinson broke the color barrier in Major League Baseball. The jitterbug was popularized by music from live bands and jukeboxes. For the first time, humans held the means to annihilate themselves at the push of a button. By the end of the decade, confrontation—a standoff between the capitalist West and the communist East—was back. This was the start of the "Cold War."

1940s Las Vegas

Las Vegas entered the 1940s much the way the rest of America did, with an uneasy uncertainty about what was happening in Europe involving Germany, Italy, and Great Britain. After America entered World War II in 1941, Las Vegas did its part by sending its sons to serve in the military. Some of them came back to glory and peace while others never came back.

The 1940s, however, were to be a momentous decade for Las Vegas in more ways than just the war. The gambling Mecca that we know today began in the 1940s. Highway 91, the road from Los Angeles to Las Vegas, was named the Las Vegas Strip, or more commonly referred to as the Strip. Former Los Angeles Police Captain Guy McAfee, who purchased the Pair-O-Dice Club on Highway 91 in 1938 and reopened it as the Ninety One Club, is credited with calling Highway 91 the "Las Vegas Strip." He said the road reminded him of L.A.'s Sunset Strip between Hollywood and Beverly Hills. Highway 91 has also been called the Los Angeles Highway, 5th Street in the city limits of Las Vegas, and Las Vegas Boulevard.

Las Vegas mushroomed overnight into the most "razzle-dazzle" gambling city in the world. The once spectacular neon signage of the 1940s grew even more spectacular during the 1950s. The years 1946 to 1967 are known as the Golden Age of Neon. "Glitter Gulch" or downtown Fremont Street, "The Strip," and Las Vegas Boulevard South became almost household names throughout the world.

Grace Hayes was considered to be the "First Lady" of Las Vegas. She was born in Springfield, Montana August 23, 1896, sang in Barbary Coast nightclubs in San Francisco, appeared as a singing comedienne on the vaudeville stage, and gravitated to Hollywood in the 1930s. She made Las Vegas her home in the early 1940s when she opened the Las Vegas Strip's most chic nightclub, the Red Rooster. Regular customers included the elite of organized crime including Benjamin "Bugsy" Siegel, who built the Flamingo Hotel and Casino, Marshall "Johnny Marshall" Ciafino, and a retinue of Hollywood movie stars of the day. Howard Hughes was known to wash out his shirts daily in the men's room. The Red Rooster nightclub on the Strip changed its name to Grace Hayes Lodge in 1952, was later renamed The

Patio and then Castaways Hotel and Casino. The site eventually became part of Mirage Hotel and Casino. The Mirage sort of stands as a shrine for Las Vegas' first lady, the nightclub hostess with the mostest.

In 1940 Union Pacific Railroad dedicated a new depot at the west end of Fremont Street, replacing the Spanish-style depot built in 1906. In 1971, Sam Boyd would open the Union Plaza Hotel and Casino on this site.

California hotelier Tom Hull built El Rancho Vegas Hotel and Casino in 1941. Located on what is now the southwest corner of Las Vegas Boulevard (The Strip) and Sahara Avenue, El Rancho Vegas was the very first resort on the Strip. It featured a neon windmill, pool, and low adobe-type bungalows, and was a popular draw for people looking for a laid-back atmosphere. Among the guests were multi-millionaire playboy Howard Hughes and mobster Benjamin "Bugsy" Siegel, who also enjoyed some of the nightlife offered in the resort's casino and showroom.

A year later the city leased property to the U.S. Army Quartermaster Corps for the development of the Las Vegas Army Air Field, renamed Nellis Air Force Base in 1950 in honor of Las Vegas Lt. William H. Nellis, a 100-mission fighter pilot who died over Germany in 1944.

In 1942, Hollywood movie producer D. W. Griffith's outpost on the Strip, the Last Frontier Hotel, was the second resort property built on old Highway 91. In keeping with the theme of the hotel, the buildings were constructed to resemble a fort setting.

The Westerner Gambling House opened in 1943 at 21-23 East Fremont Street. Benny Binion owned this downtown casino; in 1951, he also opened the Horseshoe Club.

Sophie Tucker was the first world-famous star to appear at a Las Vegas resort. Her two-week engagement in 1944 helped boost the credibility of Las Vegas entertainment.

In 1944 the Little Church of the West opened on the grounds of the Last Frontier Hotel. That same year Olympic swimming champion Buster Crabbe starred in Water Follies and a twenty-five-year-old Liberace, marqueed as Walter Liberace, made his Las Vegas debut at the Last Frontier.

Roy Rogers and Dale Evans starred in the 1946 movie, "Heldorado," filmed in Las Vegas during the 1945 Helldorado Celebration. The city parade route was modified in order to provide better lighting for the movie.

In 1946 Sammy Davis, Jr., who debuted at El Rancho Vegas Hotel the preceding year, began a long association with the Last Frontier Hotel as the star of the Will Mastin Trio.

The downtown area, the center for Las Vegas' fun and games, began to earn the appellation "Glitter Gulch" with the opening of two major casinos, Golden Nugget Gambling Hall and Eldorado Club.

America's popular crooner, Frank Sinatra, donned a Stetson to preside over the 1946 Helldorado celebration, which was witnessed by 50,000 visitors. Roy Rogers and Gabby Hayes led the parade down Fremont Street.

Jimmy Durante made his Las Vegas debut when the Flamingo Hotel and Casino opened on Highway 91 (Las Vegas Strip) in 1946. A year later, singing sensation Lena Horne made her debut at the Flamingo. At this time African-American performers weren't allowed to eat or sleep at the hotels.

The Thunderbird Hotel and Casino opened in 1948, the fourth and last hotel-casino to open on the Las Vegas Strip in the 1940s. Also in 1948, fresh from TV exposure on the Ed Sullivan Show, Dean Martin and Jerry Lewis opened at the Flamingo Hotel and time-honored cabaret star Joe E. Lewis began his reign as El Rancho Vegas' top-drawing performer.

In 1949, jazz singer Ella Fitzgerald played to packed showrooms during her Las Vegas debut at the Thunderbird Hotel.

Popular entertainers in Las Vegas during the 1940s included Jimmy Durante, Sophie Tucker, Sammy Davis, Jr., Dorothy Dandridge, Ella Fitzgerald, Ginny Simms, Ted Lewis, Vic Damone, Jack Carter, Dean Martin, Jerry Lewis, Joe E. Lewis, Sonja Henie, Frankie Laine, Peggy Lee, and Liberace.

The following five hotel/casinos opened on Highway 91 (Las Vegas Strip) during the 1940s:

El Rancho Vegas, 1941, 2700 Highway 91

Last Frontier, 1942, 3120 Highway 91

Flamingo, 1946, 3555 Highway 91

Thunderbird, 1948, 2755 Highway 91

Club Bingo, 1947, 2535 Highway 91 (This casino and nightclub evolved into the Sahara Hotel and Casino in 1952.)

The following eight casinos opened in downtown Las Vegas during the 1940s:

El Cortez, 1941, 600 East Fremont Street
Pioneer Club, 1942, 25 East Fremont Street
Westerner Gambling House, 1943, 21-23 E. Fremont St.
Nevada Baltimore Casino, 1944, 614 North Main Street
Monte Carlo Club, 1945, 15 East Fremont St.
Golden Nugget Gambling Hall, 1946, 129 E. Fremont St.
S. S. Rex Club, 1945, 128 East Fremont Street
Eldorado Club, 1947, 128 East Fremont Street
California Club, 1946, 101 East Fremont St.

Night Scene, Fremont Street. In the 1940s Las Vegas had many establishments that attracted not only the sunburned men working at the Basic Magnesium plant in Henderson and Nellis Air Force Base, but also motorists traveling through the southwest. Curious sightseers would refresh themselves at motels before taking a casual look at the various games and even courting Lady Luck. Beginning around 1943-1945, weekenders from Los Angeles, in significant numbers, began to descend upon Las Vegas to sample the pleasures that the clubs offered. Many of them thought of Las Vegas as a suburb of Los Angeles. Circa 1940s, $3-5.

Union Pacific Railroad Depot. Located at the west end of Fremont Street, the Union Pacific Depot was built in 1940, replacing the old Mission-styled depot built in 1906. This was the world's first streamlined, completely air-conditioned railroad passenger station. Typically modernistic western in motif, the structure was described by architects as one of the most beautiful in design and superlatively complete in appointments in the United States. Circa 1940, $6-8.

Old Fremont Street. Before the return of legalized gaming in 1931 and the end of prohibition, Fremont was a drab Las Vegas street. The main drag in downtown Las Vegas was named after Explorer John C. Fremont. During the next fifteen years small casinos and saloons began sprouting, but the big growth started with the opening of the Golden Nugget Gambling Hall in 1946 and the Eldorado Club in 1947. Gaining in reputation as "Glitter Gulch," Fremont Street, with wall-to-wall gaming clubs, clearly reflected the image of the budding recreation center. With these two new electrical displays, Second and Fremont Streets became the most brightly-lit corner this side of Manhattan's Time Square. Circa 1940s, $3-5.

Early Fremont Street Clubs. Mayme Stocker, who received the first Clark County gaming license in 1931, operated the Northern Club at 15 East Fremont Street in downtown Las Vegas until 1943. The site became the Turf Club during 1943 and 1944. In 1945 Wilbur Clark opened the Monte Carlo Club at this location. The Coin Castle Casino operated a popular slot machine joint here from 1970 to 1999, when it was transformed into La Bayou. Shown are the Turf, Las Vegas, Pioneer, and further down Fremont Street, the Frontier clubs. The first sign on the left side is the Boulder Club. Circa 1944, $6-8.

Dice Table.
In Nevada, legalized gambling means precise controls and constant vigilance to guarantee an honest deal, a random bounce of the dice, and an unbiased spin of a roulette wheel. For 1949 the gross revenue from gambling for the entire state was almost $41 million, with the Las Vegas area accounting for fifty-five percent. Here, several gamblers try their luck on the crap table at El Rancho Vegas Hotel. Circa 1940s, $10-12.

Playing Tango. People play tango at a casino in downtown Las Vegas. Tango was a game similar to BINGO. In the 1930s, tango was also played in Tony Cornero's gambling ships off the southern California coast and in William Harrah's Tango Club in Reno, Nevada. Circa 1940s, $15-17.

Playing Roulette. At the various gaming tables no social distinctions were observed; it was not uncommon to see a be-diamonded divorcee, a construction worker, a snappy dressed businessman, and a burly truck driver rubbing shoulders and placing bets. In this view of a roulette game both men and women were placing bets. Circa 1940s, $4-10.

Memorabilia. Gaming chips used in Las Vegas casinos opened during the 1940s. Circa 1940s, $2-150.

Popular Clubs of the Era

California Club

Phil Long opened the California Club at 101 East Fremont Street in downtown Las Vegas. Long sold the popular club and it closed in 1970. The location later became the Friendly Club in 1978 and became part of the Golden Nugget in 1983.

The California Club. Located on Fremont Street, it was across from Mint Casino and next to the Nevada Club and Lucky Casino. In this view a portion of the gaming tables can be seen and in the background a replica of Sutter's Mill, one of many unique and intriguing displays in the California Club. The Sutter's Mill was where the 1849 California gold rush started. Slot machines were located in front of this scene. Circa 1940s, $14-16.

Club Bingo

At a time when posh hostelries were beginning to enhance Las Vegas' image, the modest Club Bingo opened July 24, 1947 on Highway 91 as the city's newest gambling den. Ideally located across from El Rancho Vegas, it featured a 300-seat parlor for BINGO in addition to the usual casino games. The club was also known for its fine food.

On opening night Club Bingo raffled off a new Cadillac. The owner of a downtown Las Vegas hamburger stand won the car.

Club Bingo was a step ahead of most of its competitors in offering noteworthy talent. Dorothy Dandridge, an academy award nominee, kept Club Bingo a hot spot in the late 1940s. In 1949, comedian Stan Irwin was booked for eleven days and stayed for eleven months. He became manager of the Bonanza Room and went on to become Public Relations and Promotions director for the club.

There was a gambling incident in the casino a few months after the club opened. The casino cage had only about $800 at the time Walter Melrose, a visiting Southern California hotelman, beat the club badly at the crap table. Melrose won $17,000 playing against the clubs own shills and the club was in trouble. They simply could not pay him off. The club management found out that Melrose loved to sip Old Rarity Scotch and listen to the tune, "Mexicali Rose." The management dragged the combo that had been playing in the casino over to the crap table where Melrose was playing and had them play "Mexicali Rose" over and over again. And they made sure he was supplied with all the "Old Rarity" he could drink. As a result, Walter Melrose soon wound up owing the Club Bingo casino $17,000 instead of the other way around! That $17,000 turned the Club's financial picture around from near failure to a huge success.

The club operated until 1952, at which time Milton Prell turned Club Bingo into the famous Sahara Hotel and Casino.

Club Bingo. Opened on Highway 91 in 1947, Club Bingo was located across from El Rancho Vegas Hotel and Casino and featured a 300-seat parlor for bingo in addition to the usual games of craps, roulette, and blackjack. In 1952, Milton Prell remodeled and opened it as the swank Sahara Hotel and Casino. Circa 1940s, $10-12.

El Cortez Hotel. Marion Hicks and J. C. Grayson built the El Cortez Hotel and Casino, downtown's first major resort, for $245,000 in 1941. For a brief period in 1945, the El Cortez Hotel had several owners including underworld mobsters Benjamin "Bugsy" Siegel, Meyer Lansky, Gus Greenbaum, Moe Sedway, Davie Berman, and Willie Alderman. Circa 1940s, $6-8.

El Cortez Hotel and Casino

The El Cortez Hotel and Casino, built by Marion Hicks, opened in November 1941 on the corner of Fremont and Sixth Streets in downtown Las Vegas. It had seventy-one rooms, cost $325,000, and had a Wild West motif to compete with the first Strip hotel-casino, El Rancho Vegas. Other owners in the 1940s included Benjamin Siegel, Meyer Lansky, and Gus Greenbaum. Jackie Gaughan acquired it in the early 1980s and expanded it by adding a $12 million, fourteen-story, 200-room hotel tower.

A portion of the original hotel still stands today. The wing at the corner of Fremont and Sixth Streets remains almost entirely unchanged from the way it was on opening day, making it by far the oldest original casino in Las Vegas.

Intersection of Fremont and Sixth Streets. Like resort hotels and railroad depots throughout the west, the El Cortez Hotel and Casino, at Fremont and Sixth streets, took the rambling Spanish style indigenous to the region. The hotel's original guest rooms with their hardwood floors and tile baths are still intact and are reached via a creaky staircase just off the casino floor. In 1951, the ground floor of the El Cortez was "modernized," adding a neon canopy by Young Electric Sign Company (YESCO) and bezel-framed display windows. The exterior has remained virtually unchanged since then. Circa 1950s, $5-7.

Interior View. The beautiful El Cortez Casino afforded round the clock entertainment for visitors who wished to try their luck. An attractive bar, nightclub, and coffee shop adjoined the casino. Shown are a roulette table and craps and blackjack tables. Circa 1940s, $8-10.

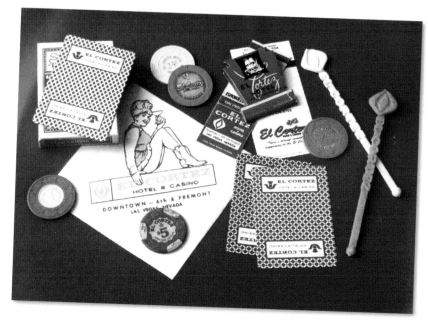

Memorabilia, El Cortez Hotel and Casino. Playing cards ($4-6), $5 gaming chip ($6-10), $1 gaming chip ($3-6), 25¢ gaming chip ($4-8), matchbook ($6-12), swizzle stick ($2-4), and napkin ($3-6). Circa 1940s.

Eldorado Club

In 1947 the Eldorado Club, located at 128 East Fremont Street in downtown Las Vegas, was opened in the Apache Hotel. Benny Binion bought the Eldorado Club and Apache Hotel and, in 1951, turned this facility into the Horseshoe Club.

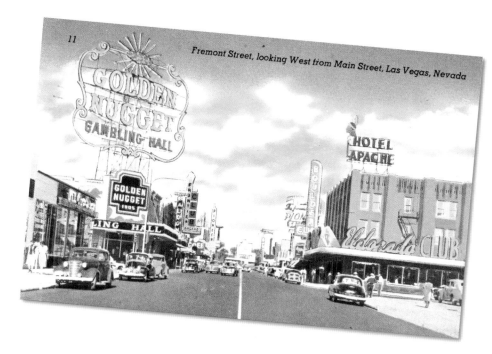

Fremont Street, Looking West from Second Street. The Eldorado Club opened in 1947 at 128 East Fremont Street across from the Golden Nugget Gambling Hall. The Eldorado Club had three crap tables, two roulette tables, a faro bank, sixty-five slot machines, and a restaurant and bar. In 1951, Benny Binion, a gambler from Texas, bought the Eldorado Club and Apache Hotel and renamed it the Horseshoe. Circa 1947, $8-10.

El Rancho Vegas Hotel and Casino

El Rancho Vegas was the first hotel built on the road that would later become the Las Vegas Strip. It was built by Thomas Hull, who owned several "El Rancho" hotels in California. El Rancho Vegas opened April 3, 1941, and at that time was located outside city limits.

The 65-room, low-rise motor inn, on the corner of Highway 91 and San Francisco Avenue (now Sahara Avenue), came complete with casino, showroom, steakhouse, swimming pool, palm trees, and lawns. Hull's El Rancho Vegas attracted the traffic coming in from Southern California, as well as locals escaping the claustrophobia of downtown's Glitter Gulch. Business boomed from the beginning, and the hotel was expanded to 125 rooms. It was the headquarters in the immediate pre-war days for all the military "brass" that visited Las Vegas to watch the progress of the construction of the Army Air Force Base (now Nellis Air Force Base) and the bored Hollywood citizenry who wanted to play and found Las Vegas a real outlet.

Some of the entertainers that performed at El Rancho Vegas were Sophie Tucker, Joe E. Lewis, Lili St. Cyr, Billy Daniels, Guy Lombardo, Nat "King" Cole, Gordon MacRae, Harry James, Gloria DeHaven, Hildegarde, Carmen Miranda, Vic Damone, Constance Moore, Hoagy Carmichael, Celeste Holme, Larry Parks, Betty Garrett, Rudy Valee, Katherine Dunham, Estellita, Jimmy McHugh, Dorothy Dandridge, Ray MacDonald, Peggy Ryan, The Kean Sisters, Jack Carson, Jeanne Gilbert, Susan Zanuck, The Ritz Brothers, Joel Grey, Beatrice Kay, Jack Haley, Denise Darcell, Luba Matina, Abbott and Costello, Benny Goodman, Yma Sumar, Martha Stewart, Lena Horne, Harry Richman, and Judy Johnson.

In March 1944, the hotel was sold to Wilbur Clark and S. P. Barbash. Two years later, they sold El Rancho Vegas to Sanford Adler and Charles Resnick, who had the hotel for a little more than a year before selling it again to Beldon Katleman. It was Katleman who, in 1960, ejected a Chicago mob figure known as John Marshall (actually Marshall Caifano) from the hotel because he was concerned about his gambling license. John Marshall was one of the first mobsters included in the Nevada "Black Book" of people not permitted in any licensed gaming establishment in the state. Within two weeks of Katleman's ejection of Marshall from El Rancho Vegas, on June 17, 1960, the hotel burned to the ground in the early morning hours. The cause of the fire was never determined. The land on which El Rancho Vegas stood was bought by Howard Hughes' Summa Corporation in the 1970s, but remained vacant for many years.

Stop at the Sign of the Windmill. In 1941, Los Angeles hotelman Thomas Hull noticed the heavy traffic on the narrow two-lane road leading out of Las Vegas for Los Angeles. He picked a spot and bought thirty-three acres at $150 an acre and built the El Rancho Vegas Hotel and Casino. For ten years, downtown Las Vegas was the center of casino action, but that trend shifted when El Rancho Vegas opened. Circa 1940s, $8-10.

El Rancho Vegas. On April 3, 1941, El Rancho Vegas Hotel and Casino opened on Highway 91, outside the city limits of Las Vegas. This was the first casino resort on what later became the Las Vegas Strip. Circa 1940s, $10-12.

Desert Setting. The first hotel-casino on Highway 91 (Las Vegas Strip), El Rancho Vegas Hotel and Casino, was a lush oasis set in the roadside desert. Circa 1941, $5-7.

Games of Chance. Popular gambling games at the El Rancho Vegas Casino were roulette and blackjack. Circa 1940s, $10-12.

El Rancho Vegas Casino. A roulette table, blackjack table, and a bank of Sun Chief slot machines at El Rancho Vegas; it was the first hotel and casino to open on the famous Las Vegas Strip. Circa 1940s, $10-12.

The "Sitting Box," El Rancho Vegas Casino. The boxman oversees the action and is the highest authority in a craps game, settling disputes about payoffs, rules, and mistakes. Circa 1940s, $5-7.

Memorabilia, El Rancho Vegas Hotel and Casino. $25 gaming chip ($100-200), $5 gaming chip ($25-50), $500 and $1,000 fantasy chip ($1-3), matchbook ($12-14), drink coaster ($1-3), napkin ($1-3), ashtray ($12-14), brochure ($1-3), swizzle stick ($2-4), and miscellaneous paper ($1-3). Circa 1940s-1950s.

Flamingo Hotel and Casino

The day after Christmas in 1946, Benjamin "Bugsy" Siegel and the toughest board of directors that anyone ever faced — Mickey Cohen, Lucky Luciano, Jack Dragna, Meyer Lansky, and Frank Costello — opened the Flamingo Hotel and Casino. It was named after the pink flamingos at the Hialeah horse track in Florida. The Luciano, Lansky, and Siegel combine had once owned a piece of the Hialeah track, and it had been a lucky spot for Bugsy. Jimmy Durante led off the entertainment with Tommy Wonder, Baby Rosemarie, the Tunetoppers, Eddie Jackson, and Xavier Cugat's band. The casino lost $300,000 in the first two weeks and closed. It reopened March 27, 1947 when the hotel portion was completed. Bugsy Siegel never lived to see this money tree take shape. He was murdered June 20, 1947 at approximately 10 p.m. in the living room of his girlfriend's (Virginia Hill) mansion at 810 North Linden Drive in Beverly Hills, California. Only minutes before Siegel was killed, three members of the mob walked into the general offices of the Flamingo and seized control.

The Flamingo, the third major hotel-casino on the Strip, had 150 luxurious hotel rooms, a health club and gymnasium, tennis and badminton courts, steam rooms, casino, restaurant and theater, a nine-hole golf course, stables with forty saddle horses, trapshooting range, and nine different shops of national prominence.

The hotel was landscaped with Oriental date palms, rare cork trees from Spain, and fifteen varieties of other fully-grown trees. Inside the hotel, besides potted plants, modern furnishings, and plush carpeting, tuxedos were the uniform of every employee. Tux-clad personnel were so much the rule that Siegel, with his violent temper, reportedly kicked a tuxedoed guest off a poolside chaise thinking he was part of the help. In Siegel's obsession with perfection, he stationed men throughout the casino to not only watch the gambling action, but to prevent guests from flicking ashes on the carpet or obstructing slot machines if they weren't actually playing.

A glittering massive marble and brass staircase, circling up from the main lobby, led to the plush Sky Room where dancing and romance were the features every evening.

Hank Greenspan, then publisher of the *Las Vegas Life* magazine, described the hotel in this way:

"To capture its sweep and grandeur you have to be conditioned by a Goldwyn set that's been dolled up by Orson Welles. This Flamingo is indeed a most colorful and amazing bird."

The 600-seat Flamingo Room had the enviable reputation of having renowned stars from the entertainment world performing at its nightly dinner and midnight shows. The entertainment roster in the early years included Ted Lewis, Ray Bolger, Jimmy Durante, Joe E. Lewis, Pearl Baily, Jerry Lewis and Dean Martin, Nat "King" Cole, Shelly Winters, Judy Garland, Ella Fitzgerald, Danny Thomas, Bobby Darin, Phyllis Diller, Bobby Vinton, Wayne Newton, and Jack Benny. Singer Lena Horne made her debut at the Flamingo, as did Bill "Bojangles" Robinson, billed as the "World's Greatest Dancer." In 1947, Siegel's hotel was becoming the hottest place in town.

The 300-seat Casino Theater in the Flamingo's lounge featured top-flight star attractions from early afternoon until dawn. The stage, the largest of any lounge, had every modern showroom device built in, allowing magnificent productions seldomly possible in a show lounge.

The Flamingo Hotel was sold to Kirk Kerkorian in 1967. It was under his ownership that the erupting flower pylon sign was erected in 1968. Kerkorian supposedly bought the hotel to train executive and casino personnel to man his gargantuan International Hotel and Casino, which was scheduled to open in 1969. To this end, he sold the Flamingo to the Hilton Corporation shortly after his new hotel opened.

Benjamin "Bugsy" Siegel.
One of the handsomest hoodlums of his day, no one who valued his life ever called Benjamin Siegel "Bugsy" to his face. "My friends call me Ben," he once snapped at a reporter. In 1944 "Bugsy" arrived in Nevada to get involved with in the Las Vegas gambling scene and build the fabulous Flamingo Hotel and Casino. One of the first hotel-casinos he purchased was the El Cortez Hotel and Casino. In late evening, June 20, 1947, "Bugsy" Siegel was shot to death as he sat reading a newspaper in the living room of Virginia Hill's mansion in Beverly Hills, California. An unknown assassin fired nine rifle shots; four of the slugs found their mark and "Bugsy" was dead at the age of 41. Siegel's murder sensationalized the Strip and firmed up Las Vegas' reputation as a risky, naughty place where main street Americans could rub shoulders with notorious mobsters. Circa 1940s, $5-7.

Hotel Flamingo, Las Vegas, Nevada

7B-H1908

Flamingo Hotel.
The Flamingo Hotel and Casino opened briefly in 1946 before closing. After its March 1947 re-opening, it became one of the Strip's most famous resorts. It was truly a showpiece, featuring 105 beautiful rooms surrounded by a health club, steam rooms, gymnasiums, tennis, badminton, squash and handball courts, stables with forty head of riding stock, a championship swimming pool, a trapshooting range, and a 9-hole golf course. This view is of the Flamingo sign with a neon flamingo on top of the pylon and the main entrance to the casino. Circa 1947, $8-10.

The Fabulous Flamingo. A view of the well-decorated swimming pool at the plush Flamingo Hotel. "Bugsy" Siegel's fourth floor penthouse suite in the Oregon Building held a dominant position over all Flamingo activities during his brief tenure as its tenant. The Oregon Building had seventy-seven rooms. Some of its staircases led nowhere, and underground passages wound through a maze of steam pipes and boiler rooms before exiting out of doors, all in an effort to foil any attempt on Siegel's life. The closets in Siegel's suite featured escape hatches that led down to a garage with a getaway car. Circa 1947, $4-6.

A "New" Flamingo. The Flamingo Hotel changed its profile in late 1953 by adding a new façade and the tallest freestanding beacon on the highway called "the champagne tower." The new look set new standards of elegance and extravagance in the desert. The tower was eight stories high and covered from top to bottom with neon rings in the shape of bubbles that fizzed all eight stories up into the desert sky all night long, like an illuminated whisky-soda tumbler filled to the brim with pink champagne. The eighty-foot high tower was the tallest freestanding sign structure on the Strip during the 1950s and helped light up the Las Vegas night sky in the 1950s and 1960s. The sender of this card wrote, "Saw and heard Pearl Bailey and Harry James and his orchestra here tonight and both were terrific." Cancelled 1958, $10-12.

Aerial View. In the 1950s most of the Las Vegas Strip was still barren desert. In this view looking north, the Flamingo Hotel and Casino is visible in the foreground, and farther along, Sands Hotel and Casino is under construction. The Last Frontier Hotel and Casino is on the left, and the El Rancho Vegas Hotel and Casino is further north. The Sahara Hotel and Casino is across from El Rancho Vegas. Circa 1952, $7-9.

Flamingo Hotel. Remodeling in 1967 gave the Flamingo a covered Porte Cochere, a sky-room restaurant, and a new, pink-flumed roadside sign. Circa 1967, $5-7.

Craps. The fastest action game in the world, gamblers root for a seven or eleven in this Flamingo Casino view. Craps provides opportunity to win big (or lose big) on every roll of the dice. At least your right arm got a lot of exercise in this game. Circa 1956, $8-10.

Eager to Play. Patrons crowd the floor of the Flamingo Casino in this photo from the 1950s. At a time when most casinos were less than 3,000-square-feet in size, table games covered most of the floor, with only a few slot machines. The sea of ties, furs, suits, and pearls on the casino floor makes it clear that gambling in Strip casinos was a dressed-up affair during this time period. Circa 1950s, $10-12.

Blackjack. Also known as "21," Blackjack is the most popular table game in most casinos, and with good reason. It's easy to play, the casino advantage is low, and the entertainment value and social interaction is high. Here, a group of friends share a game in the Flamingo Casino. Circa 1956, $5-7.

Memorabilia, Flamingo Hotel and Casino. Playing cards ($4-6), matchbook ($10-12), swizzle stick ($2-4), napkin ($4-6), and keno playing guide ($3-5). Circa 1940s-1950s.

Golden Nugget Gambling Hall

Los Angeles businessman Guy MacAfee opened the Golden Nugget Gambling Hall August 31, 1946. Formerly the Mission Saloon that opened in 1905, Golden Nugget's brightly lit 100-foot-high sign on the corner of 129 East Fremont Street was one of the most photographed signs in the world. And the 5,000-square-foot Golden Nugget building was one of the largest facilities dedicated exclusively to gambling in the world.

In July 1951, the Golden Nugget partnership changed into a corporation for tax purposes. The change made Golden Nugget the first public gaming corporation.

The gambling hall, with its mahogany bars and crystal chandeliers, reminded one of the Barbary Coast and the Virginia City at the turn of the twentieth century. Before 1958 there were nude murals behind the mahogany bars.

During the 1960s the Golden Nugget was enlarged when the Lucky Casino and Nevada Club, located just west of the Nugget, were purchased. In 1972 Steve Wynn took control, bought the Friendly Club, built two hotel towers, and turned the gambling hall into the Golden Nugget Hotel & Casino, a plush resort in downtown Las Vegas. Later the Golden Nugget purchased the hotel at 200 South First Street, formerly the Elwell Hotel (1946-1965), Pioneer Club Hotel (1966-1968), and Golden Hotel (1969-1984), and turned it into the Golden Nugget Parking Garage.

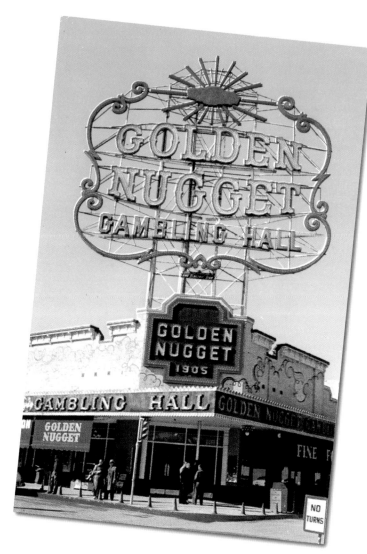

Adding Signage. A large 100-foot sign was added to the Golden Nugget Gambling Hall in 1950. Circa 1950, $8-10.

The Golden Nugget. Opened in downtown Las Vegas August 31, 1946, the date on the sign (1905) is the date of the founding of the city of Las Vegas. Circa 1946, $6-8.

Night View, Golden Nugget. The imprint on the back of this postcard reads: See the old-style west in our modern world. A place of mahogany bars, crystal chandeliers, with the genuine hospitality and old-time gaiety of the Barbary Coast and the Virginia City of fifty years ago. The sender of this card wrote, "This city is really a fabulous place. We didn't lose much money, but we had lots of fun." Cancelled 1955, $6-8.

Interior View. Shown are the nude murals located over the mahogany bar in the Golden Nugget Gambling Hall. The murals were removed in 1958. Cancelled 1950, $6-8.

Sign of the Times. In 1957 the Golden Nugget Gambling Hall sign was modified by the Young Electric Sign Company (YESCO), changing its cowboy Victorian look to neon Victorian. The large frame sign overhead remained, but it was given a pedestal with a huge bull nose of opulent Lillian Russell proportions rendered in neon. The two street facades along Fremont and Second Streets were covered for 100-feet in neon tubing; every few seconds each façade would be swept in rose and blue hues. The floriated borders of Victorian ornament were rendered in jumping neon. Circa 1957, $6-8.

Roulette Table at the Golden Nugget. Circa 1940s, $8-10.

Main Gambling Room, Golden Nugget. Shown are crap tables, a roulette table, several blackjack tables, six slot machines, crystal chandelier, nude mural, and mahogany beams and bar. Circa 1946, $14-16.

The "Bingo Room." Every day thousands played this game of chance at the Golden Nugget. Note the crystal chandeliers and painting on the wall. Circa 1940s, $8-10.

Golden Doll Slot Machine. Harold "Hap" Hancock, lead slot mechanic for Golden Nugget Casino in Las Vegas, built special conversion fronts for the machines beginning in the early 1950s; they were his own designs, and the patterns were built at the Golden Nugget. The first Golden Nugget machine was basically a Mills Golden Falls slot machine, which was replaced by two well-proportioned ladies holding genuine gold plated "golden nuggets" above their heads. The Golden Nugget boys affectionately knew these 'ladies' as "the dolls." The converted machine was officially dubbed Golden Doll, which was very popular with Golden Nugget's patrons. This machine was used in the Golden Nugget during the 1950s. *Machine is from author's collection.* Circa 1950s, $3,200-3,500.

Memorabilia, Golden Nugget Gambling Hall. Playing cards ($4-6), $5 gaming chip ($15-30), $1 gaming chip ($3-8), matchbook ($3-8), matchbox ($3-5), security patch ($8-10), ashtray ($6-8), gaming guide ($13-15), shampoo bottle ($1-3), playing card box ($6-8), cocktail napkin ($1-3), drink coaster ($2-4), swizzle stick ($1-3), keno form ($1-3), keno playing guide ($1-3), and pen ($1-3). Circa 1940s-1960s.

Last Frontier Hotel

The success of El Rancho Vegas impressed Oklahoma and Texas theater magnate R. E. Griffith so much that he started construction of the Last Frontier Hotel further south on Highway 91 (Las Vegas Strip). The hotel was constructed in the form of a rambling ranch house that was so familiar to the early Spanish Dons of southern California. The elaborate dining rooms, casino, bar rooms, and housing facilities were lined with native stone, set in place by expert Zuni Indians, brought to Las Vegas for this special purpose. It was the most magnificent gambling hall Nevada had ever seen, surpassing in splendor the plush confines of the Washoe Club in Virginia City, the Willows in Reno, and even its immediate predecessor, El Rancho Vegas.

The grand opening for Last Frontier Hotel was held October 30, 1942. In keeping with its name, a four-horse-drawn stagecoach was used to transport VIPs to the hotel from the airport and the railroad station. Headboards in the 107 guest rooms resembled large oxen yokes. Cow horns were used liberally throughout the hotel, the main showroom and dining room were decorated with Navajo artwork, and a trophy room displayed mounted game animals of the West. The forty-foot mahogany-backed bar had been removed from the old Arizona Club and installed in the Last Frontier's Gay 90's bar.

The Last Frontier Village, a re-creation of a frontier town, was built on the grounds to the north of the main complex. The buildings included a rustic chapel known as the Little Church of the West. The first of many celebrity couples to tie the knot there were Betty Grable and Harry James in 1943. The Village also contained nine hundred tons of western artifacts and offered horseback riding, stagecoach rides, and area pack trips.

A new casino was built at the front of Last Frontier Village, called the Silver Slipper Gambling Hall.

It was only natural that, with two resort hotels operating, there would be a wild contest to see which could out-do the other with elaborate floorshows. El Rancho Vegas had set the pattern for floorshows when Miss Maxine Lewis, recognized as the "entertainment queen" of Las Vegas, quit her singing role at El Rancho Vegas to become entertainment director of the hotel. She introduced such names as Donald Novis, Olive and George (modern day successors to P. T. Barnum's Tom Thumb and his wife), the Radio Rogues, Ethel Shutta, and Carmen Cavatarro.

When Griffith completed the Last Frontier, Miss Lewis followed him from El Rancho Vegas as entertainment director of the new hotel and was responsible for bringing Liberace from a complete unknown to a sparkling star.

In 1955 the Last Frontier Hotel was torn down to make room for a much larger facility, the New Frontier Hotel and Casino.

Hotel Last Frontier, the Early West in Modern Splendor, Las Vegas, Nevada

Photo by Ullom

74673

The Last Frontier. Movie theater magnate R. E. Griffith bought thirty-five acres of barren desert two miles south of Tom Hull's El Rancho Vegas Hotel and Casino and built the Last Frontier Hotel and Casino. Circa 1942, $6-8.

The Historic "Gay Nineties" Bar

Hotel Last Frontier - Las Vegas, Nevada

The "Gay Nineties" Bar. The corral out back was for horses; the corral up front was for dudes and gals. These three guests, in western attire, are enjoying the lawn in front of the Last Frontier Hotel's "Gay Nineties Bar." Circa 1940s, $8-10.

The Early West in Modern Splendor!

HOTEL LAST FRONTIER LAS VEGAS, NEVADA

The Early West in Modern Splendor. Last Frontier Hotel and Casino opened in 1942 as the first themed casino resort. Its Western theme fit the city's promotion of itself as "the early west in modern splendor." Circa 1942, $6-8.

Aerial View, Last Frontier Hotel and Casino. Note the large amount of vacant land in the vicinity of Highway 91 (the Las Vegas Strip). A Union Pacific Railroad train is in the background. Circa 1945, $7-9.

"21 CLUB" CASINO

HOTEL LAST FRONTIER — LAS VEGAS, NEV.

A NATURAL COLOR REPRODUCTION FROM KODACHROME

4B-H584

The 21 Club, Last Frontier Hotel. Shown are two roulette tables, two crap tables, three blackjack tables, and several slot machines. Circa 1940s, $12-14.

"Little Church of the West", Hotel Last Frontier, Las Vegas, Nevada

9B-H111

Little Church of the West. It was the chapel where Harry James and Betty Grable exchanged vows in 1943; Judy Garland said "I do" to Mark Herron in 1965; and where Elvis Presley slipped a ring on Ann-Margaret's finger in the 1964 film, "Viva Las Vegas." These celebrities were among more than 100,000 happy couples from all over the world who exchanged vows at the Little Church of the West, the oldest building on the Las Vegas Strip, and the first structure in Las Vegas built as a wedding chapel. For more than a half century, Little Church of the West was a fixture on the Strip—first on the grounds of the Last Frontier Hotel and for twelve years on the grounds of the Hacienda Hotel. In 1966 it was relocated to Russell Road. With its redwood interior and cedar exterior, the Little Church, which has been photographed countless times over the years, evolved into one of the most recognizable landmarks on the Strip. Other celebrities to take the plunge there were Zsa Zsa Gabor, Robert Goulet, Dudley Moore, Mel Torme, and Mickey Rooney. Circa 1940s, $5-7.

Last Frontier Village, Hotel Last Frontier, Las Vegas, Nevada

0C-H1788

Last Frontier Village. Located next to the Last Frontier Hotel, the village is a reconstruction of the main street of an old-time mining town. It contained several authentic buildings over one hundred years old and thousands of early western relics in its two museums. The Silver Slipper Gambling Hall, which was located in one of the village buildings, can also be seen in this view. Circa

Monte Carlo Club

The Monte Carlo Club opened in 1945 at 15 East Fremont Street in downtown Las Vegas, the original location of the Northern Club, which had been the first club to receive a gaming license in 1931.

Monte Carlo Club. Wilbur Clark opened the Monte Carlo Club at 15 Fremont Street in downtown Las Vegas in 1945. He later sold this club and used the profits to build the Desert Inn Hotel and Casino in 1950. Circa 1945, $6-8.

Nevada Biltmore Hotel and Casino

The Nevada Biltmore Hotel and Casino opened in 1944 at 614 North Main Street in downtown Las Vegas. The Mills Brothers premiered there in 1946.

Pioneer Club

The Pioneer Club opened in April 1942 on the southwest corner of First and Fremont Streets. It occupied a spot in downtown Las Vegas, which had also housed Beckley's clothing store during those early days. The club, which was built by Luthor B. (Tutor) Scherer, had most of the popular casino games of the day, including faro and pan. Scherer got his nickname of "Tutor" when he started tutoring his dealers, floor managers, and pit bosses in the fine art of cheating so that they could apprehend any cheats that might try their cheating techniques in his casino.

"Vegas Vic," the friendly hand-waving cowboy sign, was added to the front of the Pioneer Club in 1951. This seventy-five foot tall talking neon cowboy, which said "Howdy, Podna," became Las Vegas' most enduring image.

The club was called "New Pioneer Club" from 1956 to 1967. The Pioneer Club bought Club Bingo, which was located on the west side, and demolished it in 1983 to enlarge its casino area.

In 1968 an incomplete deck of cards was found in play during a Pioneer Club blackjack game. The owner was fined $10,000, and the club was permitted to reopen with slot machines only. Later the Pioneer Club opened with new owners.

The Pioneer Club closed June 28, 1995. The gambling casino had five different owners in fifty-three years.

Corner of First and Fremont Streets. The Pioneer Club opened in 1942 on Fremont Street in downtown Las Vegas. Circa 1942, $6-8.

PIONEER CLUB AND COCKTAIL LOUNGE
LAS VEGAS, NEVADA, CORNER FIRST AND FREMONT

Pioneer Club, One of the Big Gambling Halls, Las Vegas, Nevada

One of the Big Gambling Halls. The Pioneer Club was a big, roomy grind joint that catered to low rollers, with 25¢ craps and roulette tables, $2 blackjack, and rows of three-wheel mechanical slot machines. Circa 1940s, $6-8.

The Pioneer Club. Despite a long and storied history in downtown Las Vegas, the Pioneer Club's real claim to fame occurred in 1951 when the iconic Vegas Vic, the 75-foot-tall neon cowboy, was installed atop the casino as a promotion sponsored by the Chamber of Commerce. Vic puffed a hand-rolled cigarette, waved (when his elbow joint was working), and bellowed, "Howdy Podna, welcome to Las Vegas." Circa 1951, $6-8.

Memorabilia, Pioneer Club. Playing cards ($4-6), $5 gaming chip ($8-12), $1 gaming chip ($9-17), 25¢ gaming chip ($4-8), matchbook ($3-12), gaming guide ($10-12), and napkin ($1-3). Circa 1940s-1960s.

S. S. Rex Club

The S. S. Rex Club opened in 1945 and closed a year later. It was located at 128 East Fremont Street in the Apache Hotel. The site became the Eldorado Club and later the Horseshoe Club.

S.S. Rex Club. Underworld figure Tony Cornero shut down his gambling boat off Santa Monica, California, the *S. S. Rex*, under pressure from California Attorney General Earl Warren in August 1939, but then attempted to re-launch it on the inland sea as a club, the "S. S. Rex," in the Apache Hotel in downtown Las Vegas in 1945. It closed a year later. In 1947 the Eldorado Club opened here and in 1951 Benny Binion opened his Horseshoe Club. Circa 1946, $5-7.

Thunderbird Hotel and Casino

The fourth major hotel-casino on the Strip, the Thunderbird Hotel and Casino was owned by builder Marion B. Hicks and attorney Cliff Jones. It opened September 2, 1948. Named after an ancient Navajo legend, "The Sacred Bearer of Happiness Unlimited," the Thunderbird's motif included Native American portraits on the walls of the Wigwam Room and Navajo Room restaurants and the Pow-Wow showroom.

The 111,000 square-foot complex was the first Strip hotel-casino covered with a Porte Cochere. On top of the desert tower lookout was the Thunderbird, its talons gripped onto the tower roof. Another neon mate was perched on the roadside sign. The Navajo-style Pow-Wow dining showroom had a small stage and heavy wooden trusses over the white tablecloth covered tables.

The Thunderbird Hotel had a swimming pool with a high dive, palm trees, and lawn. This pool was billed as the largest pool in Nevada, containing 360,000 gallons of water.

In the 1950s the hotel was enlarged; a 500-seat Terrace Room, a dance floor, a new Porte Cochere, and a taller sign pole with three pennant signboards were added. In 1952 the owners of Thunderbird built the 110-room Algiers Motel to accommodate more tourists. Guests of the Algiers were given the same perks and benefits as if they were staying at the Thunderbird.

Controlling interest in the Thunderbird was actually held by Meyer Lansky and his brother Jake, a fact the *Las Vegas Sun* disclosed in a series of articles in 1955. Those articles resulted in the revocation of the Thunderbird's gaming license, although the license was finally won back after a protracted legal battle. The Thunderbird was sold in 1964 to Del Webb, who also owned the Sahara Hotel & Casino and Mint Hotel & Casino downtown. In 1972, the Thunderbird was bought by Caesars, and in 1976 sold to Major Riddle, who had owned and operated the Dunes Hotel and Casino. Riddle remodeled the hotel and renamed it "Silverbird." It remained the Silverbird until 1981 when Ed Torres (of the Aladdin Hotel and Casino) bought the hotel out of bankruptcy, remodeled it, and reopened it in 1982 as the El Rancho Hotel (not to be confused with El Rancho Vegas Hotel) and Casino. The El Rancho struggled for several years, as larger, fancier, and more fantastic hotels were built on the Strip. In July 1992, it closed.

The Thunderbird. The $2 million, 76-room Thunderbird Hotel and Casino was the fourth major resort to open on Highway 91 (Las Vegas Strip). It opened September 2, 1948. Circa 1948, $7-9.

Porte Cochere. Thunderbird Hotel was the first Strip hotel covered with a Porte Cochere. On top of the desert tower lookout was the Thunderbird, its talons gripped onto the tower roof. Another neon mate was perched on the roadside sign. Its blinking eyes caused many a motorist to gasp in wonder at its beauty. Cancelled, 1954, $7-9.

Plenty of Rooms Available. The Thunderbird Hotel's name was derived from an ancient Navajo legend—"The Sacred Bearer of Happiness Unlimited." In 1950 the Thunderbird had a total of 206 rooms and an annex. It then added a six-unit bungalow and the Casino Bar. In 1952, the owners of the Thunderbird built the 110-room Algiers Motel on the property to accommodate additional guests. Two years later the 450-500 seat Terrace Room was added. Circa 1950s, $7-9.

New Owner. In 1964, Del Webb bought the Thunderbird Hotel, adding a new façade south of the original entry as well as bringing the room count to five hundred. The 700-foot-long, free-standing sign stretching across the old wings south of the entry was the longest sign in Las Vegas; it had letters that stood out on a bed of gold light. The original Thunderbirds were replaced with an updated one created by Ad-Art. Circa 1965, $7-9.

Aerial View. An aerial shot of the beautiful Thunderbird Hotel and Casino and its spacious grounds ideally situated on the Las Vegas Strip. This picturesque hotel was world famous for its fine food and western hospitality. Another of the hotel's distinctive features was a large, 360,000-gallon swimming pool. Circa 1965, $7-9.

Westerner Gambling House

Texas gambler Benny Binion came to Las Vegas and invested in the Las Vegas Club, which was located at 23 East Fremont Street in downtown Las Vegas. After it moved across Fremont Street to the Overland Hotel, Binion sold his interest in the club and opened the Westerner Gambling House in the building where the Las Vegas Club had been previously located. Binion later sold the Westerner Gambling House to buy the Eldorado Club and Apache Hotel, where he opened the Horseshoe Club in 1951.

The Westerner Gambling House had other owners until it became Club Bingo in 1960.

The Westerner Gambling House. Opened in 1943 at 21-23 East Fremont Street in downtown Las Vegas, this casino became the Club Bingo in 1960. Circa 1940s, $6-8.

Chapter Four:
The 1950s—
The Thrilling Fifties

1950s America

The Cold War between America and the Soviet Union occurred throughout the 1950s. As the decade began, both countries had atomic bombs and the threat of a devastating nuclear war hung over the world. A race began to outgun the other side with more powerful weapons. Allied soldiers were sent to Korea to fight the forces of communism. But for many people in America, international tension was balanced by home comfort. Particularly after 1955, they enjoyed high wages, large automobiles, and home comforts like vacuum cleaners and washing machines. Inventions familiar in the modern world made their first appearance. Television became popular; "I Love Lucy" and "Gunsmoke" were hits. Teenagers chose their own fashions and music. Elvis Presley thrilled young people and shocked their elders. In January 1959 Alaska was admitted as the forty-ninth state, and in August Hawaii became the fiftieth state.

1950s Las Vegas

At the beginning of the decade the population of Las Vegas was 50,000 and there were four major hotel-casino resorts along the Strip: El Rancho Vegas, Last Frontier, Flamingo, and Thunderbird.

A lot of people feel that the 1950s was the Golden Age of Las Vegas. It was a time when the city was still relatively small but getting better known all the time. Many hotels and casinos were built during the fun-filled fifties. In 1955, the great comedian Joe E. Lewis opened his act at El Rancho Vegas Hotel with a line that best described the 1950s era:

_____

"I had a funny thing happen to me on the way to the show-room tonight; I ran into a man who wasn't building a hotel."

_____

Old Fremont Street. Fremont Street was the center of Las Vegas in the 1950s, with most of the town's most prominent casinos. The Golden Nugget Gambling Hall and Vegas Vic sign are seen on the left. Hotel Apache, Binion's Horseshoe Club, Boulder Club, and the Las Vegas Club are on the right. Circa 1951, $5-7.

Bomb Testing. This view illustrates an A-bomb cloud over the Nevada Test Site, about sixty-five miles northwest of downtown Las Vegas. Kaboom! Until 1962, all the atomic bomb tests were done in the atmosphere. Las Vegas put a stop to these aboveground tests after Aunt Helen's pot roast started to glow. Since then, all tests are done underground. Also shown are the Pioneer Club, Westerner Gambling House and Monte Carlo Casino signs on the left and the Las Vegas Club sign on the right. The Pioneer Club's neon cowboy, Vegas Vic, was the most recognizable sign on Fremont Street. Circa 1951, $3-5.

Las Vegas' Second Industry. In early 1951 Las Vegas gained a worldwide reputation for a second industry—nuclear weapons testing. America was mired in the early throes of the Cold War and President Harry S. Truman was looking for a secure stateside location to test the nation's nuclear weapons inventory. The site selected, fifty miles northwest of Las Vegas, was a vast expanse of desert surrounded by the Nellis Air Force Base bombing and gunnery range. Above ground nuclear testing was a public attraction at a test site near Las Vegas in January 1957. All-night parties were organized by Las Vegas hotels for the detonations, which could be viewed from building tops. One of the parties' highlights was the dubbing of a showgirl as "Miss Atomic Blast." Circa 1957, $5-7.

Vegas Vic. Five stories high, the spectacular sign of Vegas Vic decked out in a broad brimmed hat, bandana, and spurs, towers over the Pioneer Club. The swagger of his arms back and forth was visible all along Fremont Street and from the railroad depot. Vegas Vic started waving to Fremont Street pedestrians in 1951. *Author photograph.*

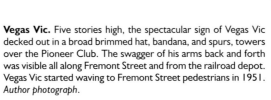

The Fabulous Strip. With the opening of El Rancho Vegas Hotel and Casino, in 1941, the now famed "Strip" reshaped the city of Las Vegas with a seemingly endless array of resort hotels and casinos. The Last Frontier, Flamingo, Tropicana, Desert Inn, Riviera, Sahara, Sands, Stardust and Dunes were but a few of the early establishments vying for tourist dollars. In this view are the New Frontier, Royal Nevada and Stardust hotel-casinos on the left and the Desert Inn and Riviera hotel-casinos on the right. In 1952 the phrase "Las Vegas Strip" became the accepted parlance for the former Highway 91 (also called Los Angeles Highway). Circa 1958, $3-5.

Las Vegas Convention Center. Opened in 1959 at the intersection of Convention Drive and Paradise Road, it was located near the famous Las Vegas Strip. At a cost of over 5-½ million dollars, it was a modern architectural phenomenon built on a desert floor. The convention center marked the beginning of Las Vegas as a business travel destination. Circa 1959, $3-5.

Memorabilia. Gaming chips used in some of the Las Vegas casinos that opened in the 1950s. Circa 1950s, $3-65.

Two years after ascending to recording nobility with gold disc Number 1, "Nature Boy," Nat "King" Cole debuted in the small but growing entertainment center at the Thunderbird Hotel in January 1950.

Wilbur Clark started off his career as a bellman at San Diego's Knickerbocker Hotel, and gradually gained enough ground to buy land along what was then Highway 91. In addition to building the El Rancho Vegas Hotel, Clark started construction on the Desert Inn Hotel and Casino. When he ran out of money, he recruited some joint partners to help him complete the project. The Desert Inn opened in 1950, but it eventually changed hands.

In 1951, the Young Electric Sign Company (YESCO) built "Vegas Vic," Nevada's largest sign to date for the front of the Pioneer Club in downtown Las Vegas. Standing seventy-five feet tall and weighing 12,000 pounds, this cowboy had articulated arms and a voice that welcomed tourists with "Howdy Podna!"

Downtown Las Vegas changed when Benny Binion turned the Eldorado Club into Binion's Horseshoe Club in 1951.

Also in 1951 Jane Russell was in town filming "The Las Vegas Story," which also starred Victor Mature and Vincent Price, and one of Las Vegas' greatest benefactors, Frank Sinatra, showcased his talent to the gambling public for the first time at the Desert Inn Hotel. Two years later, Wilbur Clark got the ball rolling for Las Vegas' major sporting image with the first annual golf Tournament of Champions at the Desert Inn Country Club.

In 1954, Hollywood's Ronald Reagan made his only Las Vegas stage appearance at the Last Frontier Hotel. That same year, the Lucky Strike Club opened in downtown Las Vegas at 125 East Fremont Street.

Last Frontier Hotel closed in 1955 and the New Frontier opened next door.

Legendary crooner Nat "King" Cole performed in the Copa Room at Sands Hotel and Casino. In 1955, in response to Cole's protests, Sands Hotel became the first Strip resort to welcome their black headliners as guests.

Gene Krupa, credited with being the originator of the drum solo, proved why he was rated the best in the country during a one-time visit in early 1955. He appeared in the Gay Nineties Bar in the Last Frontier Hotel. One of the many Benny Goodman sidemen to make significant contributions as leaders of their own groups, Krupa was supported by Eddie Shu (sax), Bobby Scott (piano), and John Dru (bass).

The Fabulous Dorseys were just one of the many first-rate acts to play in Las Vegas. At the New Frontier in late 1955, even the cowboys and their gals turned out for the smooth sound of brass and woodwinds.

The Golden Slot Casino opened in 1955 at 22 East Fremont Street. The casino closed in 1958 and the site later became the Glitter Gulch Casino in 1980 and the Girls of Glitter Gulch dancing club in 1992.

1955 was a boom and bust year for Las Vegas: the Riviera Hotel and Casino, Dunes Hotel and Casino, Royal Nevada Hotel and Casino, New Frontier Hotel and Casino, Moulin Rouge Hotel and Casino, Golden Gate Casino, and Desert Showboat Motor Inn and Casino all opened, but several of these casinos encountered financial trouble. To regulate the growing industry, the Gaming Control Board was created.

In the 1956 MGM musical, "Meet Me In Las Vegas," Dan Daily romanced Cyd Charisse; cast as a French ballerina, Charisse was making her Las Vegas debut. Jerry Colonna, Lena Horne, and Frankie Laine were guest stars in this production. The Silver Palace opened on the northwest corner of Fremont and First Streets the same year.

In 1956 the Fremont Hotel and Casino, the newest addition to downtown Las Vegas, opened with fifteen floors, making it the tallest building in Nevada. Also in 1956, fire destroyed one of Las Vegas' oldest legalized gambling clubs, the Boulder Club, on Fremont Street. In 1957, nine-year old Liza Minnelli appeared before her first Las Vegas audience with her mother Judy Garland, who called her out of the audience to join her for a couple of songs.

The "Minskys Follies" debuted January 10, 1957 at the Dunes Hotel on the Strip. The review show, imported from Paris, France, was a big hit for the next 4-½ years. The "Follies" was the first bare bosom stage show in Las Vegas

Also in 1957 the Nevada Club and Mint Casino opened on Fremont Street. In 1965 the Mint added a 26-story hotel that featured an outside glass elevator.

In 1958, the Young Electric Sign Company (YESCO) erected the largest sign in Las Vegas on the Stardust Hotel. This massive sign fascia covered the entire front of the building. It boasted thousands of flashing light bulbs and neon tubes, simulating stars and planets against a painted lunar background.

Comedy great Jack Benny premiered on the Strip in 1958 at Flamingo Hotel. The Stardust Hotel and Casino, the world's largest resort complex, opened in 1958, after four years in construction, with 1,000 rooms. Its entertainment package featured the city's first lavish production show, "Lido de Paris." A year later Las Vegas' second French-flavored extravaganza, "Folies Bergere," began its long run at Tropicana Hotel and Casino. It has become Las Vegas' longest running floorshow as the dancers are still performing in the showroom. Las Vegas began to climb to world prominence as a major convention city in 1959 with the unveiling of the Las Vegas Convention Center.

The Bird Cage opened at 100 East Fremont on the corner of Fremont and First Streets in 1958. The casino closed the following year and was incorporated into the Mint Casino.

By the late 1950s, Las Vegas had a well-established image of success and glamour. Many world-famous entertainers made their Las Vegas shows legendary and Las Vegas became "the Entertainment Capital of the World," a name by which it's still known. Popular entertainers during the 1950s included Sophie Tucker, Frank Sinatra, Helen Traubel, Peggy Lee, Betty Grable, Joe E. Lewis, Elvis Presley, Maurice Chevalier, Rosemary Clooney, Danny Thomas, Liberace, Jack Benny, Ronald Reagan, Jack Carter, Sammy Davis, Jr., Nat "King" Cole, Marlene Dietrich, Vic Damone, Judy Garland, Ray Bolger, Abbe Lane, Eddie Fisher, Ted Lewis, Edgar Bergen, Louis Prima, Keely Smith, Dean Martin, Jerry Lewis, Billy Daniels, Kitty Kallen, Margaret Whiting, Billy Eckstine, Gordon MacRae, Milton Berle, Red Skelton, Gale Storm, Spike Jones, Billie Holiday, Dinah Shore, Ginger Rogers, Earths Kitt, Abbot and Costello, Anna Maria Alberghetti, Herb Shriner, Peter Lind Hayes, Joel Grey, Tallulah Bankhead, Esther Williams, Don Rickles, Jane Powell, Noel Coward, Edie Adams, Mae West, Zsa Zsa Gabor, Lili St. Cyr, Steve Lawrence, Eydie Gorme, and George Burns.

As each hotel was opened, the entertainment names became bigger and bigger and the floorshows became more glamorous. Salaries for the stars were rocketing to astronomical heights. In 1953 screen legend Marlene Dietrich made $30,000 a week at the Sahara Hotel. At the same time the Sands Hotel paid Tallulah Bankhead $25,000 a week. A decade later, Liberace was paid $50,000 a week to perform. Many of the other 1950 entertainers were paid rates of between $5,000 and $50,000 per week for their artistry. In order to combat the rising fees of Hollywood stars, many hotel operators starting using static shows—ones that presented the same show throughout the year, changing the theme perhaps a couple of times a year. The management at Stardust Hotel imported the "Lido de Paris" show from Paris, France for its opening in 1958. The following year Tropicana introduced the "Folies Berger," another French-flavored review show.

In addition to spectacular floorshows and glamorous stars, Las Vegas also provided another form of international entertainment — the Flying Ambassadors in Blue. The Thunderbirds, the Air Force's crack precision flying team, are located at Nellis Air Force Base near Las Vegas and from there they fan out all over the world to show just what kind of pilots the U.S. Air Force has.

The official aerial demonstration team was activated in May 1953 by the national defense establishment. It was given the task of promoting a better understanding and appreciation of air power and to assist with the effective advancement of national power objectives. The Thunderbirds have accomplished their mission with a high degree of success. The flying team performs around ninety shows per year. By the end of 1963, the team had performed in 860 shows, flown the equivalent of eighty-one times around the world, and thrilled more than fifty-four million spectators in forty different countries. And, they always come home to their base just north of Las Vegas.

The following hotel and casinos opened during the 1950s on Fremont Street in downtown Las Vegas:

Horseshoe Club, 1951
Lucky Strike Club, 1954
Golden Gate Hotel and Casino, 1955
Golden Slot Casino, 1955
Fremont Hotel and Casino, 1956
Silver Palace Casino, 1956
Mint Casino, 1957
Bird Cage, 1958

The Moulin Rouge Hotel and Casino opened in 1955 at 900 West Bonanza Boulevard on the west side of Las Vegas. In 1955, the Desert Showboat Motor-Inn became the first major facility on Boulder Highway, about an eighth of a mile from the casino center in downtown Las Vegas. "Minsky's Follies of 1955" headlined the entertainment package on opening night. In 1957 this facility became the Showboat Hotel and Casino.

The following hotels and casinos opened on the Las Vegas Strip during the 1950s:

Desert Inn Hotel and Casino, 1950
Silver Slipper Gambling Hall, 1950
Sahara Hotel and Casino, 1952
Sands Hotel and Casino, 1952
New Frontier Hotel and Casino, 1955
Dunes Hotel and Casino, 1955
Riviera Hotel and Casino, 1955
Royal Nevada Hotel and Casino, 1955
Hacienda Hotel and Casino, 1956

San Souci Hotel and Casino, 1957
Tropicana Hotel and Casino, 1957
Stardust Hotel and Casino, 1958

By the end of the 1950s there were thirteen major hotel-casinos on the Las Vegas Strip. Fourteen hotels had opened. However, the Royal Nevada Hotel and Casino opened in 1955, closed in 1958, and became part of the Stardust Hotel and Casino.

1. El Rancho Vegas Hotel & Casino, April 3, 1941
2. Last Frontier Hotel & Casino, October 30, 1942
3. Flamingo Hotel & Casino, December 26, 1946
4. Thunderbird Hotel & Casino, September 2, 1948
5. Desert Inn Hotel & Casino, April 24, 1950
6. Sahara Hotel & Casino, October 7, 1952
7. Sands Hotel & Casino, December 15, 1952
8. New Frontier Hotel & Casino, April 4, 1955
9. Riviera Hotel & Casino, April 15, 1955
10. Royal Nevada Hotel & Casino, April 19, 1955
11. Dunes Hotel and Casino, May 23, 1955
12. Hacienda Hotel & Casino, October 12, 1956
13. Tropicana Hotel & Casino, April 4, 1957
14. Stardust Hotel & Casino, July 2, 1958

Popular Clubs of the 1950s

Bird Cage Casino

The Bird Cage Casino was located at 100 East Fremont Street, the northeast corner of First and Fremont Streets, in downtown Las Vegas. It opened in January 1956, was remodeled in 1959, and became part of the Mint Casino, which was located next door. This modification gave Mint Casino a corner entrance. In 1988 the Mint was incorporated into Binion's Horseshoe Club.

Bird Cage. The Bird Cage Casino, located at 100 Fremont Street in downtown Las Vegas, was open for about a year. In 1959 it closed and became part of Mint Casino. Circa 1958, $6-8.

Desert Inn Hotel and Casino

On April 24, 1950, with financial help from Moe Dalitz, Wilbur Clark opened the Desert Inn Hotel and Casino, ushering in a new era in luxurious Las Vegas desert resorts. The 300-room Desert Inn was designed by Wayne McAllister, Hugh Taylor, and Jack Lessman; done in Bermuda pink, with green trim, the buildings, constructed out of fieldstone, concrete block, and redwood, were all topped with white tile.

The Desert Inn became the fifth major resort to open on the Las Vegas Strip. Clark introduced the first 18-hole golf course in Las Vegas and in 1953 hosted the first annual Tournament of Champions golf event.

Edgar Bergen and his sidekick, Charlie McCarthy, drew the applause of opening night audiences in the Painted Desert Room (later renamed the Crystal Room); Frank Sinatra made his Las Vegas debut at the Painted Desert showroom in September 1951; and in 1954, Betty Hutton performed her "farewell engagement" at the Desert Inn.

In 1963, the Desert Inn added its first nine-story tower. In 1964, Wilbur Clark sold his minority interest in the hotel to Moe Dalitz and died of a heart attack a year later.

The Desert Inn's Crystal Showroom entertainers came from all over the globe and encompassed nearly every form of entertainment, from the irreverent patter of the Smothers Brothers to the smooth and flowing voice of Lou Rawls.

Throughout its history, the Desert Inn remained a small resort that catered to high rollers and VIPs. There were no buffets, no cheap steaks, no extravaganzas—just classy, understated luxury.

In 1966 multimillionaire Howard Hughes moved into the ninth-floor penthouse at the Desert Inn and had his own specially designed air purifiers installed, along with a hospital bed, thick black curtains on windows and balcony doors, and key locks on the elevator. Continuously drugged, the compulsive TV addict remained in bed all day, doing business only by memo and telephone.

When the Desert Inn's management asked Hughes to move out of his penthouse so they could make room for a New Years Eve party of big-money gamblers from Chicago, the multimillionaire hermit quietly purchased the hotel from Moe Dalitz for $13.25 million. After the Desert Inn purchase in 1967, Hughes continued a buying spree in Las Vegas and within a few years his Summa Corporation was the largest hotel and casino owner in Nevada.

The fourteen-story Augusta Tower was built in 1978, and shortly thereafter the seven-story Wimbledon Tower, fronting the golf course, was added. Kirk Kerkorian purchased the Desert Inn in 1987 and made it the MGM Desert Inn. ITT Sheraton purchased the hotel from Kerkorian in 1993 for $160 million. In 2000 Steve Wynn bought the Desert Inn for $270 million and built the mega-resort Wynn Las Vegas on the site.

The Desert Inn. Opening April 24, 1950, Wilbur Clark's beautiful Desert Inn Hotel and Casino was the new star on the Las Vegas Strip. It was the fifth major resort on the Strip and opened with 300 rooms. The opening entertainment acts, capping a two-day gala, included Edgar Bergen and Charlie McCarthy, Vivian Blaine, Pat Patrick, along with the Desert Inn Orchestra and the exciting Donn Arden Dancers. Moe Dalitz provided financing and Clark served as the affable public face for the Desert Inn Hotel and Casino. Shown is a view of the main entrance. Circa 1950, $6-8.

The Beautiful Desert Inn. This view contains only a portion of the Desert Inn Hotel's beautifully decorated lobby. Casual furnishings, desert stone and redwood trim defined the Desert Inn's modernized western style. Windows looked out on the swimming pool. Circa 1950, $5-7.

Tower, Desert Inn. The Desert Inn built a ten-story tower in 1963. The cloud and cactus sign that had topped the Sky Room was hoisted to the top of the new tower. The tower's one hundred rooms were expressed in an egg crate pattern of balconies and windows on east and west facades. Circa 1963, $5-7.

Sky Room Bar. The third-story Sky Room Bar in the center of this Desert Inn Hotel view was the tallest point in Las Vegas at the time. This elegant room with its mountain views was a favorite with visitors. The sweeping grandeur of the main building at this magnificent resort introduced the guest to the luxurious livery offered by the newest and largest Las Vegas hotel. Circa 1956, $8-10.

Aerial View—Wilbur Clark's Desert Inn Hotel and Casino. The Las Vegas Convention Center is in the top left of this view. The Desert Inn Golf and Country Club is behind the hotel-casino. Circa 1960s, $4-6.

Interior View. Considered to be the classiest resort in Las Vegas at this time, shown are three roulette tables in the foreground, blackjack tables, crap tables, and slot machines. The Desert Inn was the focal point of many gambling stories. One such story concerns a gambler who held the dice for twenty-eight straight passes, but walked away with a paltry $750. Little did he realize that such an occurrence was a million-to-one happening—one that could have netted him enough money to buy the state of Nevada. Had he parlayed every single bet, he would have won $289,406,976. However, the house limit would have prevented such a win, but it does make a good story. Cancelled 1953, $10-12.

Memorabilia, Desert Inn Hotel and Casino. Playing cards ($4-6), $5 gaming chip ($13-15), $1 gaming chip ($5-7), matchbook ($10-12), drink coaster ($2-4), napkin ($1-3), keno playing booklet ($3-5), keno form ($1-3), and swizzle stick ($1-3). Circa 1950s.

Dunes Hotel and Casino

Dunes Hotel and Casino opened May 23, 1955 as the eleventh major hotel-casino on the Las Vegas Strip. The opening act was TV star Wally "Mr. Peepers" Cox. His act was so bad the owners Robert Rice, Al Gottesman, Joseph Sullivan, Alexander Barad, and Jason Tarsey paid him off after only one show and sent him on his way. The $4 million property included a 200-room hotel and covered eighty-five acres. Several months later, the owners leased the property to Sands Hotel due to money problems and Dunes closed from January to May in 1956. Jake Gottleib, mob front man for Western Trucking in Chicago, bought the property and appointed another trucker from the mid-west, Major A. Riddle, as his front man.

Gottlieb Riddle & Associates were asked to share this very lucrative business with other groups in order to obtain teamster support. Points (shares) were sold to their representatives Sid Wyman, Bob Rice, Charlie Rich, Dave Goldstein, Howie Engel, and George Duckworth and they all took an active part in running the casino. They didn't get along with each other, but with all the Teamster money they needed at their disposal, they became a winning team and made Dunes the crown jewel of the Las Vegas Strip during the 1960s and 1970s.

The $4 million Dunes Hotel had a huge V-shaped pool and a thirty-foot-high fiberglass sultan standing over the entrance. At the time, there were only a few casinos on the Strip, including the El Rancho Vegas, Last Frontier, Flamingo, Thunderbird, Desert Inn, Silver Slipper Gambling Hall, and Sands. Las Vegas was in the embryonic stage, and urban sprawl consisted mainly of desert brush.

In the 1960s, The Sultan's Table and Dome of the Sea were the town's reigning gourmet rooms. The Sultan's Table had Arturo Romero and his Magic Violins—thirteen violinists who strolled through the restaurant playing for the customers. At Dome of the Sea, Kippy Lou Brinkman reigned for years as the floating harpist, playing on a small boat in the center of the restaurant.

Customers entering the Hunt Breakfast Buffet were entertained by a red-coated huntsman instead of an impersonal security guard and tourists rubbernecked when operators paged celebrities like Cary Grant. At the Top of the Dunes, nightclub patrons had a panoramic view of the valley and danced to the Russ Morgan Orchestra.

Dunes Hotel was responsible for several entertainment firsts: On September 6, 1957 the first bare-breasted show in the city, "Minsky's Goes to Paris," debuted; and in 1961, Frederic Apcar's "Vive les Girls" began a twelve-year engagement. Buoyed by its success, Dunes Hotel imported "Casino de Paris," which played from 1963 to 1981.

In the 1960s, the hotel bought 255 acres and developed the Dunes Emerald Green golf course.

In 1964 a new sign was installed at Dunes which, at 180 feet tall, was the largest in the world. It triggered a decade of sign one-upmanship with Las Vegas hotel owners.

In the 1970s, Sultan, the giant grinning man of might who once stood over the Dunes entrance like a mammoth genie, slipped from stardom to a supporting role alongside the golf course. He stood there for a decade, patches of gray starting to show beneath his turban. Then one stormy night an electrical circuit brought him down for good. Rest in peace, Sultan, you saw the best and exciting years of Dunes Hotel.

Dunes Hotel appeared in the movie, "Diamonds Are Forever," a James Bond thriller starring Sean Connery. One of the bad guys tossed one of Bond's playmates out a penthouse window in the North Tower. Luckily, the young lady landed in the swimming pool below. You can do anything in the movies, including diving into a swimming pool from twenty-four stories up.

Over the years Dunes strived to be a leader in the area of gaming, being one of the first to offer two completely different gaming areas. The Oasis Casino offered a relaxed atmosphere with lower minimum live action games. The main casino, of course, continued to offer every game of chance with higher limits available.

Dunes Hotel was sold in late 1992 to Mirage Resorts and Steve Wynn for $75 million. It closed January 26, 1993. On October 27, 1993 a quarter of a million people (including the author of this book) crowded onto the Strip to witness the implosion of the 37-year-old Dunes Hotel and Casino. Vegas-style, it went out with a bang.

When the 24-story tower tumbled to the ground about 10 p.m. as a climax to one of the greatest fireworks display ever held in America, world-renowned Controlled Demolition Inc. left its indelible mark on Las Vegas forever.

The Dunes fell slightly to the west, away from the Strip. The elaborate nighttime show used eighty-four flash bombs and 281 fire mortars. A reported $1.6 million in fireworks was rigged to last twenty-three seconds. The pyrotechnics and fireworks display was filmed for an NBC movie, "Treasure Island—The Adventure Begins." It was believed that the Dunes implosion was broadcast on every nightly news program in the country. Steve Wynn, the impresario and ringleader, had become the undoubted king of the new Las Vegas. And, he began to develop what he promised would be his next masterpiece, Bellagio, which opened on the old Dunes site to equal fanfare five years later, on October 15, 1998.

Sultan. The fiberglass Sultan brought the gigantism of downtown Fremont Street's 1951 Vegas Vic out to the Strip. Here the thirty-foot-high Sultan welcomes guests to an eighty-five-acre vacation city-in-itself. Dunes Hotel featured the world famous Arabian Room theatre-restaurant, romantic Sinbad Bar, and lovely Caliph's Court. The famous Sultan was moved in 1964 to the resort's golf course. This roadside statue overlooked Interstate 15 until the Sultan burned in the late 1980s. Circa 1955, $5-7.

Dunes Hotel. The beautiful Dunes Hotel has been referred to as the "miracle of the desert, a thousand and one delights." The hotel's impressive entrance, beautiful gardens, and casino were unsurpassed; the Arabian Room presented nightly spectacular floorshows. Circa 1955, $6-8.

Becoming a Resort. In 1961 the Dunes was turned into a resort complex when a new 24-story high-rise tower, called the "Diamond of the Dunes," opened. Dunes Hotel now had 450 rooms. For a time, the Diamond of the Dunes was the tallest building in the state. Three years later Dunes erected a 180-foot-tall sign designed by the Federal Sign and Signal Company for $250,000. The sign weighed 1,500,000 pounds, was eighty feet wide, and used several miles of neon tubing. Circa 1964, $5-7.

Aerial View. This advertising card shows an aerial view of Dunes Hotel and Casino. Buffet dinner was $2.75, Hunt breakfast was $1.75, and the Queen Elizabeth Luncheon Buffet on the twenty-fourth floor at Top of the Strip restaurant was $3.25. Cancelled 1968, $4-6.

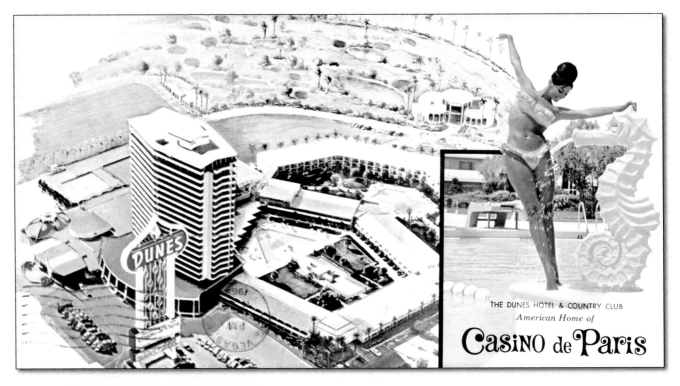

THE DUNES HOTEL & COUNTRY CLUB
American Home of
Casino de Paris

Lucky Winner. At Dunes Hotel a woman held the dice for two hours, from 2 to 4 p.m. It happened while a plane load of New York gamblers were in the hotel, and the craps table lost $300,000. The next day the story made the Paul Harvey newscast. After the craps session was over, one of the hotel's owners was being consoled by the pit boss, who told him, "Think of all the great publicity this will bring the hotel." The hotel owner growled, "Hell, that's what we've got matchbooks for!" Shown is the casino in the Dunes Hotel. Circa 1950s, $4-6.

53

The Slot Machine.
This lady is hoping to hit a jackpot on the Big Bertha slot machine at Dunes Casino. Circa 1960s, $7-9.

Bringing it Down. The Dunes Hotel and Casino was imploded October 27, 1993 to make way for new development. The event attracted national media attention and left 250,000 spectators covered in ash. *Author photograph.*

Memorabilia, Dunes Hotel and Casino. Poker room visor ($3-5), gaming instruction card ($3-5), roulette instruction card ($2-4), luggage tag ($1-3), baccarat instruction guide ($1-3), playing cards ($4-6), $25 gaming chip ($30-200), $5 gaming chip ($22-50), $1 gaming chip ($15-20), matchbook ($10-20), keno playing booklet ($3-5), and keno form ($1-3). Circa 1950s-1960s.

Fremont Hotel and Casino

The $6 million, 155-room Fremont Hotel and Casino opened May 18, 1956 at 200 East Fremont Street in downtown Las Vegas. The fifteen-story hotel was advertised as the tallest, newest, and finest in the heart of downtown Las Vegas. Downtown Las Vegas gamblers welcomed the 32,000-square-foot casino. Low gambling limits ($2 blackjack, 25¢ roulette) helped. Just 50¢ could win you a Cadillac or Ford Mustang, plus a progressive cash jackpot. The Jo Ann Jordan Trio starred in the Carnival Room lounge. Wayne Newton and his brother, Jerry, first appeared in Las Vegas at the Carnival Room in 1959.

The fourteen-story Ogden Tower, a parking garage, and the 650-seat Fiesta Theater were added in 1965. The Ogden Tower had another unusual feature for downtown—an above-ground swimming pool.

The Parvin-Dohrman group bought the Fremont in 1966, which led to bad boy Allen Glick's ownership in 1973. Glick gave the Fremont its famous face-lift, adding the block-long neon marquee for $750,000. After Glick, the Fremont changed hands several times, until the Boyd Gaming added the hotel to its holdings in 1985.

A Star in the Making. In the 1950s, Wayne Newton, at the age of 15, and his older brother, Jerry, performed in the Fremont Hotel lounge six nights a week, six hours a night, forty-five minutes on and fifteen off. It was a tough grind for them, but an incredible learning experience. After recording the hit records, "Danke Shoen" and "Mack the Knife," Wayne went on to become a Las Vegas mega-star and became known as "the King of the Strip." He played the Strip almost exclusively, averaging some thirty weeks each year. Circa 1950s, $4-6.

Fremont Hotel and Casino. Opened in May 1956 as Nevada's tallest building, it has since has been attracting tourists from all over the world. It was downtown Las Vegas' first high-rise building. The hotel sparkled in the sunlight due to quartz aggregate chips in the outer walls. It also had an aboveground swimming pool. Circa 1956, $4-6.

Memorabilia, Fremont Hotel and Casino. Roulette playing card ($2-4), gaming booklet ($1-4), gaming chips ($3-8), matchbook ($2-6), keno playing booklet ($2-4), keno forms ($1-3), and playing cards ($4-6). Circa 1950s.

Golden Gate Hotel and Casino

Hotel Nevada, located on the corner of Main and Fremont Streets, opened in 1906. It's the oldest hotel in Las Vegas. Rooms cost $1 per night and included electric lighting, ventilation, and steam heat radiators. Guests shared common bathrooms at the end of the hall. The hotel's ground floor had a lobby and a few offices, but no casino; yet there was gambling—a roulette wheel and a few poker tables—until it was outlawed in 1909.

During the 1920s, a third floor was added, and in 1931, when gambling was legalized again, the hotel was renamed Sal Sagev (Las Vegas spelled backward).

The hotel was renamed "Golden Gate" in 1955 when a group of San Francisco investors took over the hotel and opened a 9,090-square-foot casino. In 1959 the Golden Gate introduced shrimp cocktails to Las Vegas at a bargain price, and the appetizer quickly became the signature offering of the hotel. In 2008, the price of a shrimp cocktail jumped from 99¢ to $1.99.

Golden Gate Casino.
In 1955 a group of men from San Francisco opened the Golden Gate Casino in the Sal Sagev Hotel. This popular casino had most forms of gambling including craps, keno, roulette, blackjack, and slot machines. Circa 1955, $6-8.

Hacienda Hotel and Casino

The $6 million, 266-room Hacienda Hotel and Casino opened on the southern end of the Las Vegas Strip (almost two miles south of the other Strip hotels) at 3950 Las Vegas Boulevard South in October 1956. Warren "Doc" and Judy Bayley, owners of a chain of California motels, built the hotel.

The Hacienda Hotel catered to the family market with several pools and a go-cart racetrack for kids. In the early 1960s Bayley, who was a pilot, maintained a fleet of thirty DC-3 and DC-4 airplanes to bring customers from California. "Hacienda Holiday" billboards saturated highways in Southern California. The Hacienda had a private 9-hole par-3 golf course, a lagoon-size swimming pool (the largest in Nevada) and sunbathing area, and showroom.

Doc Bayley died in 1964; his wife, Judy, took over the Hacienda and ran it till she passed away in 1971.

In 1958 the Hacienda had a special room rate: one or two people for $3. In 1971 this same offer was available, but it also included a champagne breakfast, buffet brunch, champagne party, a ten-spot keno ticket per person, and forty lucky nickels per room.

In 1980 the Hacienda opened an eleven-story addition with three hundred rooms. It had ten buildings on forty-eight acres, and also was home to one of Las Vegas' oldest wedding chapels, the Little Church of the West, which originally belonged to the Last Frontier Hotel.

The Hacienda Hotel featured a new magician, Lance Burton, in "A Magical Journey," in the Fiesta Showroom. Burton started his Las Vegas performances as a fifteen-minute act in Tropicana Hotel's "Folies Bergere." He's currently performing at the Monte Carlo Hotel and Casino.

The Hacienda expanded from 740 to 1,140 rooms in 1991. Four years later, Circus Circus Enterprises purchased the 39-year-old resort for $80 million so the company could expand southward on the Strip from its Luxor and Excalibur properties. On December 1, 1996 the doors to the Hacienda were closed to the general public. Later, on New Year's Eve, the Hacienda implosion was broadcast in a ninety-minute live telecast.

The hotel buildings are gone; however, Hacienda's old forty-foot sign featuring a neon cowboy atop a horse became the centerpiece of the Neon Museum in downtown Las Vegas.

The Mandalay Bay Hotel and Casino now occupies the site of the old Hacienda Hotel.

Hacienda Hotel. In June 1956 the 266-room Hacienda Hotel opened on the Strip without a casino. Six months later the casino opened. The first major promotion by the hotel-casino was called the "Hacienda Holiday" and offered a deluxe room for $16, plus $10 dollars in gaming chips upon check-in. Circa 1950s, $6-8.

Little Church of the West. For twelve years, this picturesque marriage chapel, "Little Church of the West," was located on the grounds of the Hacienda Hotel. It was formerly located on the Last Frontier Hotel property. The chapel was built of California redwood and was an authentic replica of a little church built in a pioneer town in California. More celebrities have been married here than any other place in the world. It was also the only building on the Las Vegas Strip to be listed on the National Register of Historic Places. *Author photograph.*

Hacienda Hotel and Casino. Located on the southern end of the Las Vegas Strip, two miles from the closest Strip resort, Hacienda was the first resort seen by people driving to Las Vegas from California. During the hot summer months, people tended to stop at Hacienda Hotel first. Hacienda Hotel was noted for its Spanish-style lobby with a loud waterfall that greeted guests entering the front door. Circa 1960s, $4-6.

Having a Wonderful Time. A busy crap table at Hacienda Hotel and Casino is shown. Craps is the fastest action gambling game in the world. Circa 1960s, $5-7.

Playing Roulette, Hacienda Hotel and Casino. Circa 1960s, $5-7.

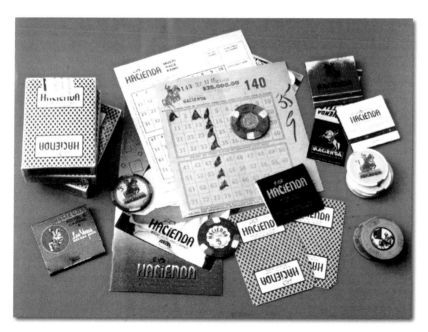

Memorabilia, Hacienda Hotel and Casino. Playing cards ($4-6), matchbook ($5-7), $5 gaming chip ($15-100), $1 gaming chip ($10-15), and keno form ($1-3). Circa 1950s-1960s.

Historic Neon Sign. After the old Hacienda Hotel palomino and caballero neon sign was removed from its original home in front of the hotel, it sat in a dusty lot behind the Young Electric Sign Company (YESCO) plant for several years along with Aladdin's Lamp, the Silver Slipper, and Caesars Palace letters. Later, sign company workers installed new bulbs and wiring and repainted the sign. On November 13, 1996 it was put atop a sixteen-foot-high pole and became a major part of the Neon Sign Museum on Fremont Street in downtown Las Vegas. The horse and rider sign was the first exhibit in this downtown museum that features historic neon signs. *Author photograph.*

The Horseshoe Club

Benny Binion, a gambler from Dallas, Texas, purchased the Apache Hotel and Eldorado Club in 1951 and changed the name to Binion's Horseshoe Club. The Eldorado Club was located at 128 East Fremont Street, on the corner of Second and Fremont Streets, inside the Apache Hotel.

The Horseshoe Club was the first casino in downtown Las Vegas to have carpeting on the floor.

Benny was almost always accessible, sitting at the corner table wearing a cowboy shirt with gold coins for buttons and no tie. He put a million dollars – one hundred $10,000 bills – on display at the Horseshoe Club; visitors enjoyed having their photographs taken in front of this display.

After the Horseshoe Club opened Binion had to serve a term in prison for income tax evasion. He sold the Horseshoe to a multimillionaire friend, Joe W. Brown, while he was away and bought it back when he returned to Las Vegas. After buying back the Horseshoe Club in 1960, Benny renamed it Binion's Horseshoe Hotel and Casino.

The old Mint Hotel and Casino, next door, was acquired by Binion in 1988 and made part of the Horseshoe Hotel. The Horseshoe now occupied a city block in downtown Las Vegas, from First to Second Streets, on Fremont Street.

Horseshoe Hotel was long famous as a casino with no house limits. The Horseshoe once lost a single bet of $770,000 on a Crap's Don't Pass line. The gambler, William Lee Bergstrom, was escorted out to his car with two filled suitcases. The gambler subsequently bet other large sums, always winning, and later brought in one million dollars—which he bet and lost on one toss of the dice. From the beginning, Binion's welcomed big bets.

Horseshoe Hotel was home to the "World Series of Poker." "Nick the Greek" Dondolas first approached Binion with the idea for a high-stakes poker marathon between top players. Binion agreed, with the stipulation that the game be open to public viewing. The competition, between "Nick the Greek" and the legendary Johnny Moss, lasted five months, with breaks only for sleep. Moss ultimately won about $2 million. As Nick lost his last pot, he rose from his chair, bowed politely, and said, "Mr. Moss, I have to let you go." Later, Binion recreated the battle of poker giants, which evolved into the annual World Series of Poker that was held at the Horseshoe until 2005.

Binion died in early 1990 at the age of eighty-five. His statue, on horseback, sits at Ogden Avenue and Casino Center Boulevard.

At midnight March 10, 2005, Binion's Horseshoe became Binion's Hotel and Gambling Hall.

Horseshoe Club Opens. In 1951, gambler Benny Binion from Texas was granted a casino operators' business license and purchased the Apache Hotel and Eldorado Club in downtown Las Vegas for $160,000. He renamed it the Horseshoe Club, a name everyone associated with good luck. The Eldorado Club came with three crap tables, two roulette tables, a faro bank, sixty-five slot machines, and a restaurant and bar. Circa 1951, $6-8.

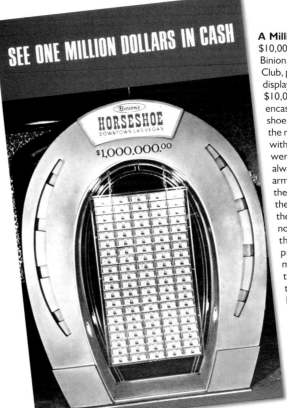

A Million Dollar Display. One hundred $10,000 bills comprise this display. Benny Binion, the founder of Binion's Horseshoe Club, purchased all of the bills shown in the display from banks before the issuance of $10,000 bills was discontinued. The bills, encased in an eight-foot golden horseshoe, were put on display in 1954. All of the money was behind bulletproof glass, with an attached alarm system. There were surveillance cameras that were always monitoring the display as well as armed security guards close by. Due to the heavy security on all of these bills, there was never an attempt to steal the money or break the glass. Another note of interest is that 62,632 bills of this particular denomination were printed between 1928-1934. The majority of bills remaining in circulation appeared in this display. Visitors to Binion's Horseshow Casino could have their picture taken from 4 p.m. to midnight daily. Most people had never even seen a $10,000 bill, let alone one hundred of them in the same location. Circa 1952, $1-3.

Doing Time. Shortly after Benny Binion opened Binion's Horseshoe Club, he had to serve four years in prison for income tax evasion (1953-1957). While in prison, he sold the club to his multimillionaire friend, Joe W. Brown, and after he was released, he bought it back from Brown, renaming it Binion's Horseshoe Hotel and Casino. The Horseshoe was a family operation. Benny Binion trained his sons, Jack and Ted, by having them deal every game in the casino and work their way up through pit boss. Circa 1960, $5-7.

The Best Gamble. Binion's Horseshoe Hotel and Casino gained a reputation for offering the best gamble in town. For the next fifty years, Binion's Horseshoe was regarded as the one true gambling hall in Las Vegas willing to accept any wager. In fact it was an early high-stakes poker game that took place at the Horseshoe that sparked the idea for the Horseshoe's annual "World Series of Poker." Circa 1960s, $4-6.

An "Extraordinary" Slot Machine. It was Mills Novelty's luxury "game of the future," introduced in 1934 for presentation at the Chicago World's Fair. This industrial exposition was a showcase for futuristic design and these ideas were reflected in this new modern slot machine. The "empire builder" type styling of the "Extraordinary" Model was the immediate center of attention wherever it was presented, and it was another styling "first" for Mills Novelty Company. Mechanically, the "Extraordinary" had all the latest features, with the new magnetic slug rejecter and anti-jam, horizontal coin escalator; the self loading jackpot and reserve jackpot display with the regular 150 coin jackpot (machine paid) and super 200 coin jackpot (casino paid). The "Extraordinary" has a highly polished cast aluminum front trimmed in royal blue. This machine was used in the Horseshoe Casino in downtown Las Vegas in the 1950s. *Machine from author's collection.* Circa 1950s, $3,200-3,500.

Memorabilia, Binion's Horseshoe Club. Gaming guide ($13-15), playing cards ($4-6), matchbook ($6-12), napkin ($1-3), keno playing booklet ($2-4), keno form ($1-3), gaming chips ($4-20). Circa 1950s-1960s.

Lucky Strike Club

Milton Prell opened the Lucky Strike Club in 1954 at 117 East Fremont Street between the Golden Nugget Gambling Hall and Nevada Club. The casino was famous for its large vertical sign that read "BINGO" and a minor with a gold pan next to it. (Prell later opened Mint Casino in downtown Las Vegas and Sahara Hotel and Casino on the Strip.) The club closed in 1963 and reopened as the Lucky Casino. In 1967 it was incorporated into the Golden Nugget Gambling Hall.

The Lucky Strike Club. Located in downtown Las Vegas between the Golden Nugget Gambling Hall and the Nevada Club, and across from the Boulder Club on Fremont Street, the Lucky Strike Club's huge vertical BINGO sign was hard to miss. The sender of this card wrote: "I'm enjoying my trip very much. Naturally we had to enter some of these places. Saw Betty Grable and Harry James at a lovely nightclub." Cancelled 1956, $3-5.

Mint Hotel and Casino

In 1957, Sahara Hotel owner Milton Prell built the Mint Casino, located at 100 East Fremont Street, between the Bird Cage Casino and Binion's Horseshoe Club. Two years later, the Mint bought the Bird Cage Casino, incorporating it into its facility and giving it a corner entrance. Del Webb bought controlling interest and in 1964 and added a 26-story hotel tower featuring an outside glass elevator and the Top of the Mint steakhouse and dance lounge. The glass elevator slid up and down the outside of the Mint, offering riders a breathtaking view of the sparkling downtown Las Vegas Casino Center, the Strip, and the towering mountain ranges In the background. The 300-room tower had a "Sky Deck" swimming pool.

Located at the "Top of the Mint" were the Ambassador Room and the Embassy Room Lounge. The Ambassador Room, one of Las Vegas' finest restaurants, featured one of the largest steaks in town – over thirty ounces of porterhouse steak – for less than $5 dollars. At the romantic Embassy Room Lounge visitors danced, sipped cocktails, and took in the breathtaking Las Vegas skyline.

The casino was large, spacious, and friendly. It also offered visitors a free "behind-the-scenes" tour, thus showing the side of the casino very few "outsiders" had ever seen before.

Binion's Horseshoe Hotel and Casino purchased the Mint in 1988 and incorporated it into the Horseshoe.

Memorabilia, Mint Hotel and Casino. Playing cards ($4-6), roulette chip ($2-4), fantasy chip ($2-4), matchbook ($10-12), and swizzle stick ($1-3). Circa 1950s-1960s.

An Elevator View. In 1965 the Mint Casino added a 26-story hotel with an outside glass elevator. An elevator ride provided riders a breath-taking view of the sparkling downtown Casino Center, the Strip and the towering mountain ranges in the background. Circa 1965, $4-6.

One-Armed Bandits. A colorful scene in the Mint Casino: row after row of mechanical slot machines. Circa 1960s, $4-6.

Mint Casino. Located next to the Horseshoe Club on Fremont Street, it opened in 1957. The Mint pioneered new sign imagery by breaking away from the dated streamline pylons of the Boulder and Las Vegas clubs. Three-dimensional, sculptural, and complex in animation, it was stunning and unique signage. The Mint's spectacular three-dimensional sweep became one of the eye-catching graphics on Fremont Street. Circa 1957, $3-5.

Moulin Rouge Hotel and Casino

The 1940s and 1950s were the segregated years when most Las Vegas hotels and casinos would not serve African American patrons. Max Schwartz opened the Moulin Rouge Hotel and Casino May 24, 1955 at 900 West Bonanza Road, a short distance west of the downtown casino area. The hotel-casino hoped to attract wealthy black customers from eastern states.

The Moulin Rouge gained national attention when it made the cover of *Life* magazine. It was the first interracial hotel and casino in Las Vegas.

During the hotel's first weeks the "Tropi-Can-Can" floor show featured the young dance team of Maurice and Gregory Hines and a cast of dancers assembled by producer Clarence Robinson, who had staged shows at the original Moulin Rouge in Paris, France. The great jazz artist Benny Carter and his band provided the music. Performers and stars like Lionel Hampton, Dinah Washington, and Les Brown played to packed houses.

With former heavyweight champion Joe Louis as part owner-host, Moulin Rouge quickly became a hot spot for big name entertainers and celebrities who gathered at the club in the wee hours of the night and early morning. Among the popular entertainers who frequented the club were Frank Sinatra, Nat "King" Cole, Sammy Davis, Jr., Harry Belafonte, Tallulah Bankhead, Gregory Peck, Dorothy Lamour, Bob Hope, Milton Berle, Louis Armstrong, Dean Martin, George Burns, Gracie Allen, Kay Starr, Jack Benny, and Mary Livingston.

Moulin Rouge closed after only six months of operation for a variety of reasons, among them under-capitalization and mismanagement. The "whites-only" casinos were losing customers to the upstart, and they pressured Moulin Rouge into shutting down.

In 1960 casino owners agreed to end segregation — the agreement was signed at the Moulin Rouge site in recognition of its pioneering efforts. The hotel was placed on the National Register of Historic Places in 1992.

An attempt was made in 1997 to resurrect the Moulin Rouge, however, it failed. In May 2003, an arson fire destroyed much of the Moulin Rouge.

Moulin Rouge Hotel and Casino. Opened from May to October of 1955, Moulin Rouge was the first club to break the color barrier in Las Vegas. Regrettably, prior to 1960, African Americans weren't allowed to gamble, dine, or stay at Las Vegas hotels and casinos—except during the brief time Moulin Rouge was open. Moulin Rouge was located on 10.5 acres of land and had a swimming pool, casino, cocktail lounge, theatre-restaurant, and 105 rooms. Circa 1955, $6-8.

Breaking the Color Barrier. Moulin Rouge Hotel and Casino was frequented by all races, but was built to accommodate a growing African American population not welcome at many Las Vegas hotels and casinos. Joe Louis, former heavyweight-boxing champion of the world, was part owner of Moulin Rouge. However, after putting his heart and soul into the business, even the "Brown Bomber" couldn't make it last the twelve rounds. Moulin Rouge finally went down for the count. Sadly, after its addition to the National Register of Historic Places in 1992, Moulin Rouge was damaged by fire on May 29, 2003. Circa 1955, $3-5.

New Frontier Hotel and Casino

On April 4, 1955 the Last Frontier Hotel rode off into the sunset and the New Frontier Hotel and Casino dropped whole from high orbit in its place to be the eighth major hotel-casino to open on the Las Vegas Strip. The New Frontier Hotel had a Stardust-like outer-space theme. Chandeliers in the shape of men from outer space, flying saucers, and spinning planets hung from raspberry glace and Daphne-pink ceilings. The hotel had the Planet dining room, the Cloud 9 cocktail lounge, and the Venus Theater. Elvis Presley made his Las Vegas bow at the New Frontier Hotel in 1956—the same year Judy Garland made her world debut as a nightclub performer at the New Frontier. In 1966 the New Frontier Hotel had the tallest sign in the world—over 184-feet tall.

The New Frontier Hotel became the Frontier Hotel and Casino in July of 1967. Multimillionaire Howard Hughes purchased the Frontier Hotel six months later for $14 million. Margaret Elardi, who had owned casinos in downtown Las Vegas and Laughlin, Nevada, purchased the Frontier Hotel from Hughes' Summa Corporation in 1988. The Frontier Hotel was imploded in 2007.

New Frontier Hotel and Casino. Crash Corrigan and his party of Hollywood celebrities arrived at the New Frontier Hotel and Casino, where the spectacular Venus Room offered nightly show productions. The hotel's Cloud 9 Lounge and Planet Room were unique and indescribably beautiful, providing twenty-four hour relaxation and amusement. Circa 1955, $6-8.

Riviera Hotel & Casino

The Riviera Hotel & Casino was the first high-rise hotel on Las Vegas' famous Strip. The Riv, as the locals called it, was the ninth major hotel-casino built on the Strip. The official hostess for the opening night ceremonies was Hollywood movie star Joan Crawford. The opening act in the Clover Room was a young man who had worked his way up through the lounges—Mr. Showman himself, Liberace. Later he introduced Las Vegas to a young singer named Barbra Streisand. At that time Liberace was the highest paid entertainer in Las Vegas. A few years later Streisand opened at the International Hotel (now the Las Vegas Hilton).

The big boys behind the Riviera were the Chicago and Florida mobs. For Chicago it was Sam "Moony" Giancana (Frank Sinatra's Godfather) with Meyer Lansky and Associates from Florida. Gus Greenbaum fronted the operation for the two syndicates. Greenbaum was later murdered in Phoenix, Arizona along with his wife.

The Riviera Hotel had nine stories and 350 rooms on twenty-five landscaped acres. Built at a cost of $8.5 million, the hotel was a radical departure from the sprawling, one- and two-story ranch style hotels that had preceded it along Highway 91 (Las Vegas Strip). The soaring complex resembled a Miami, Florida resort. The L-shaped building was one of the first to use elevators, and from the moment guests arrived at the massive stone and glass entrance and were met by a doorman that looked like a French Legionnaire, they were surrounded in European splendor.

In what was regarded as one of the most lavish openings in Las Vegas history, the Riviera threw open its doors to the public April 21, 1955.

The Riviera Hotel was famed for its varied entertainment. Headliners included Dean Martin, Debbie Reynolds, Carol Channing, Merv Griffin, Mitzi Gaynor, Harry Belafonte, Kathryn Grayson, Orson Wells, Dinah Shore, Phil Silvers, Milton Berle, Dorothy Dandridge, Mamie Van Doren, Dorothy Lamour, the McGuire Sisters, Patti Page, Marlene Dietrich, the Mills Brothers, Dennis Day, Johnnie Ray, Jonathan Winters, Ginger Rogers, George Gobel, Ray Bolger, Kenny Rogers, Liza Minnelli, and Frank Sinatra. On August 4, 1958, hundreds upon hundreds of anxious fans went to see Red Skelton. Countless had to be turned away.

In 1960 the Riviera Hotel changed the Clover Room's name to Versailles Theater. Other entertainers that appeared here included Bob Hope, Buddy Hackett, Eddie Fisher, Cyd Charisse, Sid Caesar, George Burns, Red Buttons, Tony Bennett, and Louis Armstrong. Engelbert Humperdinck debuted at the Riviera in 1969, and Paul Anka made his debut here in 1981.

The Riviera Lounge was a favorite stopping place for all Las Vegas regulars. Here they were apt to see such glittering names as Totie Fields, Jack Carter, Jan Murray, or Shecky Greene.

Over the years, the Riviera Hotel had many ups and downs, many different owners, and offered many different kinds of entertainment including "Splash," a popular music and dance production, "An Evening at La Cage," and "Crazy Girls."

The First High-Rise.
On April 21, 1955, with a total of nine stories, Riviera Hotel and Casino became the first high-rise building on the Las Vegas Strip. Liberace, along with his 23-piece orchestra, opened the new $10 million Riviera Hotel as its first headliner, with actress Joan Crawford serving as official hostess. The grand opening attracted worldwide attention. An avant-garde fashion designer named Christian Dior created Liberace's dazzling white tuxedo, and the Riviera's Clover Room Theater was draped with platinum gray velour under a jet-black ceiling, illuminated by starlight constellations. In addition to the Riviera Hotel, this view also shows the Thunderbird Hotel and Casino, Algiers Motel, and Sahara Hotel and Casino. Circa 1950s, $3-5.

Riviera Hotel and Casino. Widely known as one of the leading entertainment centers of Las Vegas, among the stars to grace the Riviera's Clover Room during the 1950s were Hollywood luminaries Zsa Zsa Gabor, Mickey Rooney, Marlene Dietrich, Red Skelton, Dinah Shore, Harry Belafonte, Ginger Rogers, and Milton Berle. Circa 1950s, $3-5.

Memorabilia, Riviera Hotel and Casino. Playing cards ($3-5), $5 gaming chip ($8-10), $5 baccarat chip ($10-12), $1 gaming chip ($3-5), 50¢ gaming chip ($4-6), matchbook ($1-6), keno playing booklet ($2-4), baccarat playing booklet ($2-4), keno form ($1-3), and pen ($1-3). Circa 1950s-1960s.

Casino Area, Riviera Hotel. In 1955, most forms of gambling were table games like blackjack, craps, roulette, baccarat, chuck-a-luck, and wheel of fortune. A few slot machines are shown across the back wall. Circa 1955, $8-10.

Royal Nevada Hotel and Casino

The early 1950s were boom times in Las Vegas. Four new resorts opened on the Strip within a few weeks in 1955: the Riviera, Dunes, New Frontier, and the Royal Nevada Hotel.

On April 19, 1955 Royal Nevada Hotel and Casino opened as "The Showplace of Showtown, USA" and became the tenth major hotel-casino to open on the Strip. The opening night entertainment was provided by opera star Helen Traubel in the hotel's magnificent Crown Room. The "Queen of the Met" sang her heart out for Crown Room patrons. The opening was an overwhelming success. The night before, soldiers stationed nearby were treated to a pre-opening party.

Royal Nevada's debut was book ended by the births of the Riviera Hotel, which opened April 15, and Dunes Hotel, which opened May 23. The Moulin Rouge Hotel opened in West Las Vegas the day after the Dunes.

Four major hotel-casinos opened within two months. All of that action drew the attention of the national press, and the Royal Nevada took full advantage of the spotlight. Its lounge hosted a number of well-known entertainers, such as the Dukes of Dixieland, which included Liberace's brothers Fred and Frank. The showroom pioneered the concept of bringing shortened Broadway musicals to the Strip with a production of "Guys and Dolls," which reunited its original Broadway stars, Robert Alda, Vivian Blaine, and Sam Levene

Royal Nevada was the first hotel on the Strip to introduce all-you-can-eat prime rib at its Chuckwagon in August 1957. The price was $1.50.

Mattress queen, Jean Armstrong, was featured on a raft of mattresses in the Royal Nevada Hotel pool during a Sealy Mattress convention.

During the 1950s there were too many new casinos and too few customers. The Royal Nevada Hotel only stayed open until March 1958. The Stardust Hotel and Casino, located next door, annexed the Royal Nevada Hotel in 1959 and made the casino part of Royal Nevada part of its convention center. The building that contained Royal Nevada's rooms became the Pool Wing of the Stardust. The former Royal Nevada swimming pool may have been more obscure than the Stardust's larger pool, but that probably didn't bother the savvier tourists who knew the "Lido" showgirls liked to swim nude to avoid tan lines.

Royal Nevada Hotel and Casino. American Indians in full dress express their approval of the newly opened Royal Nevada Hotel and Casino in 1955. The magnificent Crown Room not only offered a spectacular setting for some of the world's best entertainers, but also presented a dazzling, nightly display of the world-famous Dancing Waters, an indoor fountain display with 38-tons of cascading water that was accompanied by colorful lights and music. Plagued with financial problems from the beginning, the hotel survived only a short time. Circa 1955, $5-7.

Swimming. The beautiful patio and Olympic-sized swimming pool at the Royal Nevada Hotel and Casino; an oasis of luxury and cool comfort. After Royal Nevada closed and became part of Stardust Hotel and Casino, Stardust high-rollers stayed in the Royal Nevada wing and shared the pool with "Lido" showgirls. Circa 1955, $5-7.

Sahara Hotel and Casino

The story of the Sahara Hotel and Casino began with the old Club Bingo on dusty Highway 91. With a bright neon sign illustrating giant bingo cards, Club Bingo opened on a rainy July 24, 1947. Its main attraction was a 300-seat bingo parlor. The club had a smattering of other casino games.

The founder of the Sahara Hotel and Casino was Milton Prell, a Los Angeles jewelry mogul who guided the building and growth of the Sahara. Del Webb's construction company built the hotel. They are still there.

With the "Wizard of Oz's" scarecrow, Ray Bolger, kicking up his heels on the Congo Room stage, the Sahara Hotel opened its doors October 7, 1952 and became the sixth major hotel-casino to open on the Las Vegas Strip.

Prell wanted his "jewel of the desert," as he called the Sahara, to capture the flavor of Africa. Hence the major facilities of the hotel were given exotic names like "Congo Room," "Caravan Room," and "Casbar Lounge." The décor of these rooms also echoed the theme with oversize models of African warriors and spears, and caravan desert scenes. Camel statues were erected in front of the hotel.

In 1953, screen legend Marlene Dietrich made her Las Vegas debut at the Sahara Hotel for $30,000 a week—the biggest payment for talent to date.

In 1952 Louis Prima and Keely Smith, with Sam Butera and the Witnesses, established themselves as perennial favorites in Sahara's lounge, the Casbar.

The Sahara Hotel's main showroom, the Congo Room, featured many of showdom's greatest stars. Performers on the Sahara entertainment bill included Donald O'Conner, Connie Francis, Robert Goulet, Don Rickles, Johnny Carson, Eleanor Powell, Mae West, George Burns, Nelson Eddy, Red Skelton, Esther Williams, Sonja Henie, Ann Blythe, Ida Lupino, Dan Dailey, Victor Borge, Fernando Lamas, Jeanette MacDonald, Anna Maria Alberghetti, Helen Traubel, Fred Waring, Billy DeWolfe, Tony Bennett, Delores Gray, Bob Crosby, and Ken Murray.

In 1963, Elvis Presley and Ann Margaret filmed segments of "Viva Las Vegas" in the hotel. In the following year, the hotel's entertainment director booked the Beatles for two shows at the Las Vegas Convention Center. The Beatles stayed at the Sahara Hotel.

The Sahara Hotel owners built the Mint Casino in downtown Las Vegas in 1957. Del Webb purchased controlling interest in both properties in 1961. A fourteen-story, 200-room tower was added to the Sahara in 1966, just after the downtown Mint Hotel rose to twenty-six stories, making it the tallest building in Nevada, with its sky-deck swimming pool. In 1968, a 24-story, 400-room tower was added to the Sahara Hotel. A third tower of 26-stories, 575 rooms, and a convention center were added in 1988; and two years later, a 600-room tower was also added.

By 1990 the Sahara Hotel had 2,100 rooms, including one hundred suites. In 1995, William Bennet purchased the Sahara for $193 million and immediately began expanding the hotel. He added a 170-foot onion-shaped dome that sits atop an eighty-foot-high port cochere. The structure cost $4.6 million, including $900,000 special lighting. Also added was a $15 million racecar simulation. The casino area was expanded from 24,000 to 95,000-square-feet, increasing the table games to fifty-one and the machines to 2,000.

Sahara Hotel and Casino. Called "The Jewel of the Desert" by its builder and owner Milton Prell, the Sahara opened in October 1952 across from the El Rancho Vegas Hotel and Casino on the Strip. Opening night entertainment featured Ray Bolger, the scarecrow from the "Wizard of Oz," with his dance, song, and comedy routine, and singer Lisa Kirk. Circa 1952, $6-8.

A New Casino. The Sahara Hotel and Casino, with its African theme, quickly became a success. Circa 1950s, $12-14.

Signage. A 127-foot-high vertical roadside sign was designed and installed by Young Electric Sign Company (YESCO) in 1959. Circa 1960s, $4-6.

Exterior View. In this first exterior photo of the Sahara Hotel and Casino, entertainment director and Las Vegas comedian Stan Irwin, shown in front of the high-finned Cadillac, helped show off the new 200-room pleasure mart. Cancelled 1958, $5-7.

Sahara Tower and Skyscraper. This view of the Sahara Hotel and Casino shows the fourteen-story Sahara Tower, built in 1959, and 24-story Sahara Skyscraper, built in 1963. Cancelled 1966, $4-6.

Memorabilia, Sahara Hotel and Casino. Playing cards ($4-6), $100 gaming chip ($30-60), $5 gaming chip ($8-20), $2.50 gaming chip ($5-7), $2 gaming chip ($10-12), $1 gaming chip ($3-5), $20 gaming plaque ($30-40), matchbook ($1-2), drink coaster ($4-6), cocktail napkin ($4-6), keno playing booklet ($3-5), baccarat playing booklet ($3-5), swizzle stick ($1-3), pen ($1-3), keno form ($1-3), and shampoo bottle ($1-3). Circa 1950s-1960s.

Early view, Sahara Casino. Shown are roulette and blackjack tables and, on the right, a row of slot machines. This view illustrates that the majority of casino games were table games with only very few slot machines. Circa 1952, $12-14.

Sands Hotel and Casino

Jackie Freedman, "Doc" Stacher (an associate of Meyer Lansky), Frank Costello, and Joey Adonis, along with a group of Texans, built the Sands Hotel & Casino. Comedian Danny Thomas, with an All-Star line-up that included Billy Eckstine and Jane Powell, performed in the showroom on opening night, December 15, 1952. The owners took Jack Entratter out of the mob-owned Copacabana Night Club in New York City and made him the entertainment director. Entratter assembled the most famous stable of stars to ever appear under one roof. The Sands was the home of the famous Rat Pack (Dean Martin, Sammy Davis, Jr., Joey Bishop, Peter Lawford, and Chairman of the Board, Frank Sinatra).

The Sands Hotel, the seventh major hotel-casino to be built on the Strip, was designed by Hollywood architect Wayne McAllister and consisted of two hundred rooms housed in five two-story Bermuda-modern style buildings. These structures featured a unique "Vermiculite" tile roof that was used extensively in the tropics to provide cooler temperatures. The five buildings, all named after famous American racetracks, were arranged in a semi-circle around a half-moon shaped swimming pool.

McAllister also designed the Sands Hotel signboard that loomed like a giant egg-crate grid. It was unusual for architects to also design signs. All night long, its sizzling incandescent bulbs started off like a fuse, racing their way up and around the dynamic script lettering—S-A-N-D-S—repeating in red neon and white chasers against the black desert sky.

The Sand's entertainment director Entratter helped put Las Vegas on the map. His extensive contacts with celebrities and members of the national press kept the Sands and the city in the news. On the stage of the famed Copa Room, home of "The Most Beautiful Girls in the World," superstars such as Danny Thomas, Jerry Lewis, Jimmy Durante, Debbie Reynolds, Carol Burnett, Nat "King" Cole, Judy Garland, Paul Anka, Van Johnson, Wayne Newton, Jack Benny, Red Skelton, and "The Rat Pack" made regular appearances. The spectacular Copa Room showroom sat 395 and featured a series of nine sculptured-metal, Brazilian carnival figures.

In the 45,000-square-foot casino, warm earth tones were enhanced by expensive copper lighting fixtures. The Silver Queen Bar and Cocktail Lounge was decorated with various Nevada scenes by muralist Allan Stewart. The casino included table games, a sports' and race book, a keno lounge, and slot machines.

Three modernistic pylons, hewn from rough Italian marble, provided a striking front entrance to the hotel. A line of contemporary stone columns arched from the entrance to the rear of the building, framing the pool and parking areas. Thus the hotel's décor reflected the spirit of its slogan—"A Place in the Sun."

During the 1940s and 1950s African Americans were not allowed to stay in the Strip hotels or play in the casinos. But they were allowed to appear in the main showroom provided they left by the back door and stayed on the west side of town. The Sands Hotel once drained its swimming pool because singer Lena Horne's child swam in the pool.

It wasn't long before the Sands Hotel had many more rooms and suites located in ten garden buildings bearing an equestrian theme, which complemented Las Vegas' "Wild West" feel: Arlington (41 rooms), Belmont (38 rooms), Santa Anita (30 rooms), Triple Crown (40 rooms), Hialeah (47 rooms), Bay Meadows (40 rooms), Hollywood Park (42 rooms), Churchill Downs (77 rooms), Delmar (101 rooms), and Aqueduct (81 rooms). Verdant lawns, towering olive and palm trees, and bright desert flowers surrounded each building.

In July 1967 Frank Sinatra's plans to buy the Sands Hotel, his favorite stomping and singing ground, were scuttled when Howard Hughes beat him to the punch and snatched up the Sands. Hughes' people cut off Sinatra's credit at the gambling tables and wouldn't return his calls, and the singer, who claimed to have helped "build the hotel from a sand pile," blew his lid and pushed a table over on a 275-pound pit boss. In turn, Sinatra lost two of his front teeth.

After Howard Hughes owned the Sands, the addition of a striking eighteen-story tower, with 207 rooms, immediately identified the Sands Hotel as a contemporary trendsetter. Its upper-floor rooms were some of the classiest in Las Vegas, with rich wood appointments, sliding glass doors onto balconies, and incomparable views.

Hughes' Summa Corporation sold the Sands (and the Desert Inn) to Kirk Kerkorian in 1988 for $161 million. Sheldon Adelson was the next and last owner of the Sands Hotel. In 1990 the Sands Expo and Convention Center opened and was expanded to 1,006,396-square-feet in 1994.

On June 30, 1996, after forty-four years of continuous operation, Adelson closed the resort and announced plans to build the Venetian Hotel mega-resort on the Las Vegas Strip site. The Sands was consigned to history when it was imploded to make way for the Venetian Hotel and Casino. On December 30, 2007, an extension of the Venetian Hotel was opened on the old Sands Hotel site. The 3,066-room, 90,000-square-foot

Palazzo Hotel and Casino gives the conjoined properties a total room count of 7,128, forming the largest hotel and resort complex in the world, including two casinos totaling more than 210,000 square feet, almost one million square feet of retail stores, and 2.3-million square feet of meeting, convention, and exhibition space. The formal opening on January 17, 2008 included a fireworks display, champagne toast, and a performance by Motown legend Diana Ross and of the Tony Award-winning Broadway musical "Jersey Boys."

A Leader in the Gambling World. Since its opening the Sands Hotel and Casino established itself as a leader and innovator in the gambling world. The game baccarat was introduced in Nevada in 1959 at Sands Casino. Cancelled 1955, $8-10.

Sands Hotel and Casino. Shown as it first opened on December 15, 1952, Sands is the seventh major hotel-casino located on Highway 91 (Los Angeles Highway and later, the Strip). Circa 1952, $8-10.

Sands Hotel Tower. Sands Hotel and Casino's seventeen-story circular tower, designed by architect Martin Stern, was part of a $9 million renovation completed in 1965. Circa 1960s, $8-10.

Gambling Attire. Suits, ties, and cocktail gowns were standard attire among an earlier generation of Las Vegas Strip casino gamblers. This view was meant to accentuate Strip casinos' elegance compared to the rustic, western ambience of downtown casinos. Illustration of Sands Casino from a show program. Circa 1960s, $8-10.

Playing Blackjack, Sands Hotel and Casino. Circa 1953, $5-7.

Slot Machines. A 1950s view of the Sands Casino shows a small bank of slot machines played by well-dressed men and women. These "one-armed bandits" were representative of the conventional three-reeled mechanical slot machines common at the time. Circa 1953, $5-7.

Baccarat. Gamblers play baccarat at Sands Hotel and Casino. Note, at this time, paper money was used when playing. Circa 1960s, $7-9.

Memorabilia, Sands Hotel and Casino. Cup ($1-3), playing cards ($4-6), $5 gaming chip ($10-12), $1 gaming chip ($3-5), matchbook ($2-12), gaming guide ($3-5), drink coaster ($2-4), napkin ($1-3), keno playing booklet ($3-5), keno form ($1-3), pen ($1-3), baccarat playing guide ($1-3), and magnet ($1-3). Circa 1950s-1960s.

San Souci Hotel and Casino

The San Souci Motel opened in 1942 at 3320 Highway 91 (later the Las Vegas Strip). In 1957 the motel was enlarged and opened as the San Souci Hotel and Casino. Three years later a larger San Souci Hotel opened with one hundred air-conditioned rooms, swimming pool, and restaurant. In 1963 the San Souci was converted into the Castaways Hotel and Casino, a popular Strip facility until 1987 when Steve Wynn purchased it and turned the site into a parking lot for his Mirage Hotel and Casino.

Showboat Hotel and Casino

The Desert Showboat Motor Inn, built in the shape of a Mississippi Steamboat with paddlewheel and smokestack and located at 2800 East Fremont Street (Boulder Highway) about an eighth of a mile from the downtown casino center, opened in 1955. "Minsky's Follies of 1955" headlined the entertainment package on opening night. In 1957 this facility became the Showboat Hotel and Casino.

The $2-million, 200-room Showboat Hotel was owned by William Moore of the Last Frontier Hotel and J. Kell Housells, a longtime downtown juice man. The casino was managed by Moe Dalitz, along with others, at the Desert Inn Hotel. The Showboat was located a long way from the downtown action and had a hard time attracting out-of-town customers. The hotel-casino eventually found its niche with bowling and bingo.

In 1959 a 24-lane bowling alley was built and the hotel hosted the first Las Vegas Open, one of seven Professional Bowlers Association (PBA) events at the time. The event attracted low rollers from around the country. The Showboat had a 500-seat bingo parlor where it was possible to win $5,000 in a single bingo game. The Showboat also had a casino, restaurant, a kiddie's playroom, a miniature golf course, an "Olympic size swimming pool, and at the end of the gaming casino was the Mardi Gras Room that featured outstanding entertainment. The hotel also offered golf privileges at two Las Vegas championship golf courses.

The Showboat Hotel expanded in 1963, got a facelift in 1968, added a nine-story, 250-room hotel tower in 1973 and again in 1975. By 1979 the Showboat was the third largest bowling center in America with 106 lanes.

In 2000 the Showboat became Castaways Hotel and Casino. In 2004 Castaways was purchased by Station Casinos and was later imploded.

Showboat Hotel and Casino. Opened in 1957, it was only a short distance from downtown Las Vegas. In 1959 a 24-lane bowling alley was added to the hotel. Circa 1950s, $6-8.

A Unique Resort. The Showboat Hotel and Casino was one of Las Vegas' unique resort hotels where visitors were greeted with the fabulous illusion of a great 1840 Mississippi riverboat steaming across the Nevada desert. The Showboat's 100-room hotel, 18,000-square-foot casino, and great showroom offered a maximum in comfort, convenience, and fun. Circa 1950s, $6-8.

The Showboat Casino. Shown are crap, blackjack, and roulette tables, and mechanical slot machines. Circa 1957, $10-12.

Memorabilia, Showboat Hotel and Casino. Security patch ($3-5), key holder ($1-3), playing cards ($5-7), dice ($3-5), $5 gaming chip ($10-20), $1 gaming chip ($3-5), matchbook ($3-15), and keno form ($1-3). Circa 1950s-1960s.

Silver Palace Casino

In 1956 Silver Palace Casino opened at 32 East Fremont Street, at the corner of First and Fremont Streets, in what had been a drugstore in downtown Las Vegas. The Silver Palace closed in 1964 and became a chain of slot machine casinos: Carousel (1964), Sundance West Casino (1976), Sassy Sally's Casino (1979), and is now the Mermaid's Casino.

The Silver Palace. Opened in 1956 at 32 Fremont Street, it was formerly home to the Las Vegas Pharmacy. This downtown casino offered blackjack, craps, roulette, and slot machines. The restaurant offered a top sirloin dinner for $1.79. The location later became the Carousel (1965-1974), Gambler's Hall of Fame (1974-1976), Sundance West (1976-1980), Sassy Sally's (1980-1999), and, currently, Mermaids. Circa 1956, $12-14.

Silver Slipper Gambling Hall

The Silver Slipper Gambling Hall and Casino actually began as the Golden Slipper, which was built in 1942 and held its grand opening September 1, 1950 at the portals of the Last Frontier Hotel's Western Village. The Village would lure 6,000 to 10,000 people a day to the show, casino, false-fronted museums, covered wagons, gift shops, steam engines, and other artifacts. Shortly after it opened, the name was changed to the Silver, which eventually took over the Village.

With the Golden Nugget Gambling Hall in downtown Las Vegas, management of the Golden Slipper became convinced that Silver Slipper would be a better name. There were quiet hints of title infringement. However there was a sawdust business on Boulder Highway that already had that name. To solve the problem, Beldon Katelman, owner of the Golden Slipper, bought the Silver Slipper, closed it, and renamed the Golden Slipper the Silver Slipper.

In addition to the casino, the Silver Slipper had a popular burlesque showroom and an always-packed restaurant, which was the first Strip eatery to offer a 69¢ breakfast between the hours of 11 p.m. and 7 a.m.

During the 1950s taking photos in a casino was close to impossible. The casinos just didn't want tourists snapping pictures of their customers gambling. The Silver Slipper was the first casino to let this author take photographs of customers and dealers playing craps and blackjack. However, no pictures could be taken in the showroom.

The burlesque shows, starring longtime Las Vegas comedian Hank Henry, solidified the Silver Slipper Gambling Hall's reputation as "a hangout." Frank Sinatra, a friend of Henry's, and the rest of the Rat Pack made the Silver Slipper the "in place" for several years. Many of the stars on the strip would rush over to the Silver Slipper after their last show to catch the late show and see who was going to show up that night and clown around on stage in the burlesque skits. Can you imagine Frank Sinatra, Dean Martin, Sammy Davis, Jr., Jack Benny, Danny Thomas, Milton Berle, Joey Bishop, Red Buttons, Joe E. Lewis, and Red Skelton all on stage at the same time? That's the way it was in those days, when Las Vegas was a small friendly "fun" town.

Purchased in 1968 by Howard Hughes for over $5 million, the Silver Slipper was a popular casino until Margaret Elardi bought it in 1988 and turned it into a parking lot for the Frontier Hotel and Casino. With the wrecker's ball, nearly four decades of memories vanished. The casino and all the trimmings returned to dust.

The Silver Slipper. This gambling hall opened on the grounds of the Last Frontier Village at 3100 Las Vegas Boulevard South (Las Vegas Strip) in 1950. The Silver Slipper was home of Barry Ashton's "Wonderful World of Burlesque." A stage full of beautiful girls and no cover; show times were 10 p.m., 12:30 a.m., and 2:45 a.m. The popular Silver Slipper restaurant offered breakfast for 69¢, lunch for $1.49, dinner for $1.97, and buffet for $1.57. What a bargain! Circa 1950s, $7-9.

Memorabilia, Silver Slipper Gambling Hall. Cap ($6-8), $100 fantasy chip ($1-3) 1$ gaming chip ($15-20), matchbook ($6-8), playing cards ($4-6), gaming guide ($4-6), keno playing booklet ($2-4), and keno form ($1-3). Circa 1950s-1960s.

Stardust Hotel and Casino

Before Tony Cornero, Admiral of the Gambling Ships off the California Coast, could complete his dream palace, the Starlight Hotel on the Strip, across from the Desert Inn Hotel, he had a heart attack and died at 11:17 a.m., July 31, 1955 playing craps at the Desert Inn. The mob took over, finished constructing the hotel, and opened the Stardust Hotel and Casino July 2, 1958. The new owners were Chicago's Tony Accardo, Johnny Roselli, Murray "The Hump" Humpreys, and Jake "Greasy Thumb" Guzik. The front men were John Factor of the Factor Cosmetics family, aka "Jake the Barber," and Johnny Drew, an old Al Capone mobster. Moe Dalitz from the Desert Inn was in the background, and eventually took over complete control. Dalitz's criminal activities went back to the prohibition era. He had gambling interests throughout the country.

The Stardust Hotel and Casino had 1,032 rooms (largest in the world), a 16,500-square-foot casino (largest in Nevada), and a landmark electric sign (largest in the world). The Stardust quickly became known as one of "the spots." With its top entertainment, excellent reputation, and large size, the Stardust – and its world famous sign – became a symbol of Las Vegas. The resort was billed as a "City-within-a-City." Stardust Hotel was the fourteenth major hotel-casino to open on the Las Vegas Strip.

The entertainment at the Stardust Hotel started with the first major French spectacular, "Lido de Paris," appearing in Las Vegas' largest dinner theater on one of the biggest stages in the world. Direct from the internationally acclaimed Lido Club in Paris, France, the show boasted a cast of one hundred dancers that did justice to the town's largest showroom. On the basketball court-size stage the audience also saw the bustling sexy hub of Paris, the colorful South American countryside, the land of the Aztecs, the sinking of the Titanic, the explosion of the Hindenburg, the San Francisco earthquake, the explosion of a Texas oil field, the eruption of Mt. Fujiyama, and a massive waterfall that covered the entire stage. The Lido was the first show to introduce nudity to the American nightclub scene in a manner that was not burlesque. The show was one hour and forty-five minutes of nonstop excitement, including a dazzling array of color, lighting effects, costumes, music, and choreography. Lido de Paris enjoyed a 32-year run, some 22,000 performances before an estimated 19 million patrons. The final show was February 28, 1991. Going to Las Vegas and not taking in the Lido or one of the other elaborate production shows would be like going to New York without seeing the Statue of Liberty or going to Orlando without visiting Magic Kingdom.

Behind the Stardust Hotel was the city's only first-run drive-in movie theater. In 1960, the resort added a 4,800-square-foot screen and installed a speaker system that contained the latest stereophonic sound technology.

In 1959, the Stardust absorbed the ill-fated Royal Nevada Hotel next door, adding three hundred rooms and a convention center. The Royal Nevada had opened in 1955 and closed in 1958.

From 1959 to 1964 the Royal Nevada wing was where the Stardust put up its high rollers, who shared the private pool with Stardust's showgirls, who were also housed in the Royal Nevada wing. In 1964, this pool was opened to the public and the resort completed a nine-story, 176-room Stardust Tower, replacing half of the bungalow rooms and bringing the total number of rooms to 1,470. This would be the largest room count in Las Vegas for the next five years, until the International Hotel and Casino opened. The following year, a new 188-foot-tall sign was unveiled, costing $500,000. Its effect, at night, was mesmerizing. Its constellation of neon and incandescent bulbs made it appear that lights were sprinkling from the stars, showering down upon the sign.

The late 1970s saw tremendous growth elsewhere on the Strip, and by the 1980s the Stardust had fallen into a state of disrepair. Throughout the years the Stardust was troubled with skimming operations and mob control. When the highly reputable Boyd Group bought the Stardust Hotel in 1985, the hotel was finally free of mob influence. The Boyd Group turned Stardust into one of the most exciting hotel-casinos on the Las Vegas Strip. With its brand new 32-story, 800-room distinctively colored hotel tower, the Stardust not only had over 2,500 rooms, but a dominant position on the Las Vegas skyline. With 85,000-square-feet of casino space, Stardust was now one of the largest gaming halls in the country.

The casino had six crap tables, forty-four blackjack tables, ten poker tables, forty progressive pai gow poker tables, three Caribbean Stud poker tables, a keno lounge, several baccarat tables, two Let-It-Ride tables, a 250-seat Race and Sports Book, and 1,600 slot, keno, and video poker machines.

For a short time (1987-88) the Olde-Tyme Gambling Museum was located in the Stardust. The museum housed one of the world's largest collections of gaming memorabilia consisting of some of the finest existing examples of early American gaming craftsmanship. Items from the late 1880s through the bell slot machines of the 1940s were on display. The museum began as a gesture on the part of the Boyd Group toward preserving the history of Las Vegas gambling.

The Stardust became famous for its familiar friendliness as for its mob connections. In the 1995 movie "Casino," Robert DeNiro played a character inspired by the finely tailored Frank "Lefty" Rosenthal, who ran the resort in the mid-1970s.

Over the years, big name entertainment continued to be a signature Stardust Hotel feature. In 1999, Wayne Newton was signed to an unprecedented deal: a ten-year contract worth a reported $25 million per year. However, Newton ended his run in April 2005.

The Stardust Hotel and Casino closed at noon November 1, 2006. The Bobbie Howard Band led the last casino patrons out the front doors in a conga line while playing "When the Saints Go Marching (Out)." After forty-eight years of dazzling highs and controversial lows, the Stardust cashed in its chips.

On March 13, 2007, at 2:30 a.m., the two Stardust towers were imploded simultaneously. The tallest tower was the tallest building ever imploded on the Strip. It took eight weeks to clear the property of debris and prepare it for the next mega-resort that would be built here. When the Stardust Hotel towers were imploded, it ended a long sordid saga in Las Vegas' colorful past.

Greetings. This card of the Stardust Hotel and Casino boasted: "some 40 acres of gardens and architectural splendor" designed to meet visitors' "every need and comfort." In 1963 a room at the Stardust Hotel could be had for as little as $6, which prompted some guests at other hotels to rent rooms there just to be able to buy tickets to the "Lido de Paris" show. Stardust Hotel guests were always allowed to purchase tickets for the show. Circa 1963, $5-7.

Stardust Hotel and Casino. The biggest hotel-casino to be built on the Strip during the 1950s, Stardust was created for low-end gamblers by Tony Cornero, who built a resort around $5-dollar-a-day rooms and customers with $5 a day to gamble. Circa 1959, $5-7.

New Signage. In 1965 Stardust Hotel replaced the old circular sign with a $500,000 roadside sign. At night, incorporating neon and incandescent bulbs in an animation sequence, light fell from the stars, sprinkling from the top of the 188-foot-tall sign down over the Stardust name. It was a noted landmark on the Strip. Circa 1960s, $4-6.

Memorabilia, Stardust Hotel and Casino. Dealer apron ($5-10), playing cards ($4-6), $5 gaming chip ($8-20), $1 gaming chip ($4-10), matchbook ($4-12), key holder ($1-3), cocktail napkin ($1-3), keno playing booklet ($3-5), keno form ($1-3), roulette guide ($1-3), swizzle stick ($1-3), and pen ($1-3). Circa 1950s-1960s.

Tropicana Hotel and Casino

The $18-million, 300-room Tropicana Hotel and Casino, the thirteenth major resort-casino to be built on the Strip, opened April 4, 1957. It was initially so exquisite that it earned the nickname, "Tiffany of the Strip." Its sixty-foot tulip-shaped fountain in the center of a 110-foot-diameter pool stood as a landmark on the south end of the Las Vegas Strip for many years.

Frank Costello, the "prime minister of organized crime" on the East Coast, was the man behind the scenes. On May 2, 1957 Costello was shot in the head – but not killed – by Vincent "Chin" Gigante, a soldier in another New York family. In Costello's pocket was a note that read, "Gross casino wins as of 4-26-57: $651,284." A cashier at the Tropicana Hotel had written the note. Costello claimed it was his laundry ticket.

World famous from the day it opened, the plush desert resort sat on more than seventeen acres. Eddie Fisher and Monte Proser's Tropicana Review performed on opening night. The resort had one of the largest swimming pools in Nevada, several tennis courts, and an outstanding 18-hole champi-onship golf course.

Departing radically from the design of many other Strip hotels, the Tropicana incorporated distinctive features that created sightseeing attractions and attracted hundreds of persons daily who merely walked through the structure to marvel at its beauty. Standout features of unusual nature included the spacious public areas that totaled over 155,000-square-feet. They were incorporated in the expansive lobbies, foyers, peacock alleys, lounges, television room, casino, bars, theater restaurant, dining rooms, and shops. The landscaping was also an item of beauty. Over $1 million was spent on trees, roof gardens, flowers, and rock and tropical gardens.

In the wonderful whirl of entertainment, the Tropicana introduced its spectacular Theater Restaurant, a steeply-tiered showplace with horse-shoe-shaped rows that featured multiple stages, complete theatrical facilities, Izenour lighting, and Altech sound. Appearing twice nightly in the Theater Restaurant (main showroom) was the famed French-produced show "Folies Bergere," which was introduced in 1959. The show carried on the tradition, started in nineteenth-century Paris, of using Can Can dancers. The "Folies" has earned the reputation of being one of the finest and most exciting shows on the Las Vegas Strip. Its international beauties, lavish costumes, specialty acts, sets, and breathtaking productions made it a must for all visitors. The "Folies Bergere" show is as popular today as it was on opening night.

Other stars that have appeared in the Tropicana showroom include Ernie Kovac, Gene Kelly, Helen O'Connell, Donny and Marie Osmond, Ann-Margaret, and Peggy Fleming.

From dusk to dawn, top name entertainment was the bill of fare in the popular Blue Room Lounge. Such greats as Pete Fountain, Louis Armstrong, Helen O'Connell, Julie London, Erroll Garner, and George Shearing often appeared there.

The Tropicana Hotel changed hands several times in the 1970s. After disclosure of underworld involvement, a series of owners oversaw the deterioration of Tropicana's aura, until the Ramada Corporation purchased it in 1979 and immediately restored the property with much of its original glory. Ramada redesigned the casino in art nouveau-style, adding a million dollar, 4,000-square-foot leaded stained glass dome and 28-color carpeting. Fifty-five-thousand square yards of carpeting was manufactured on looms found only in a small town in England.

A high point of the Tropicana was the leaded-stained glass ceiling of the casino dome by interior designer Tony Devroude. It was billed as a copy of the main dome of the Hyberian Bank building in San Francisco, which collapsed in the earthquake of 1906. Judson Studios in Pasadena, California manufactured the reproduction stained glass in the dome. It's suspended on pneumatic shock absorbers to withstand building vibrations from the air-conditioning; the ceiling remains stationary and the building vibrates around it.

The Ramada Hotel chain added another hotel tower with eight hundred rooms and a lavish water park that included two floating blackjack tables in the pool.

Today Tropicana Hotel and Casino is surrounded by several mega-resorts/casinos and remains in the center of a very popular Las Vegas Strip area.

Aerial view, Tropicana Hotel and Casino. Like many of the early resorts in Las Vegas, hotel rooms were built in a two or three story "motel" style around the swimming pool area. High-rise towers came much later. When Tropicana Hotel opened, the population of Las Vegas was about 55,000. Tropicana Hotel was the next to last fanciest, and most expensive, of the Strip hotels built in the 1950s. Circa 1957, $6-8.

Water Fountain. A spectacular water fountain marked the approach to the $18 million Tropicana Hotel and Casino, which opened April 4, 1957 on the Las Vegas Strip. The hotel brought modern design to Western hospitality with friendly service through its beautiful rooms and exquisite public areas, highlighted by the exciting Theatre Restaurant where famous stars appeared. There was around the clock entertainment in the Showcase Lounge. Circa 1957, $5-7.

Tropicana Hotel and Casino. Truly a showplace of the world with luxury accommodations, beautiful casino, big name entertainment, large swimming pool, golf course, and country club. For five decades the Tropicana Hotel has showcased one of the most popular production shows in America, the famous "Folies Bergere." Circa 1959, $5-7.

Chapter Five:
The 1960s—
The Fun-Filled Sixties

1960s America

The 1960s was a decade of rapid scientific and technological progress and huge social change. It was a decade of student revolutions and "flower power." America and the Soviet Union took the Cold War into space, indulging in a race through the stars to the moon; there was also an intensification of Cold War conflicts throughout the Middle East. To promote international friendship, President John F. Kennedy established the Peace Corps in 1961. His assassination in 1963 stunned the nation. In 1965 American ground troops were deployed for active combat in Vietnam. The Beatles captivated the nation and "Star Trek" debuted. It was a decade of rebellion. Young people everywhere rose against the Establishment—demanding not just peace, but a world radically remade. On July 20, 1969, history was made as the entire world watched Neil Armstrong and Edwin Aldrin become the first people to set foot on the moon. "The Eagle has landed!" There wasn't anything that we could not do!

1960s Las Vegas

The 1960s were the heyday of Las Vegas when it leaped to the attention of people worldwide. A lot of that attention can be attributed to one man and one group of people: Frank Sinatra and his Clan. The "Rat Pack"—Sinatra, Dean Martin, Sammy Davis, Jr., Peter Lawford, and Joey Bishop—entertained at the Sands Hotel in the 1960s. Las Vegas bathed in the media limelight afforded by this group of entertainers.

The Strip's first resort, El Rancho Vegas Hotel and Casino, was destroyed by a spectacular fire June 27, 1960. Located across the road from the Sahara Hotel, El Rancho Vegas was never rebuilt.

In 1960 the Frank Sinatra film, "Ocean's 11," was filmed in Las Vegas. The premise of this popular movie was to blow up the electrical towers feeding power to Las Vegas. When all the lights would go out, and before backup power could be generated, the "Rat Pack" would clean out the vaults of the Desert Inn, Flamingo, Riviera, Sahara, and Sands hotels. The movie was set during the Christmas holidays, but was filmed during the summer.

"Vive les Girls," a long-running mini-spectacular show, debuted at the Dunes Hotel in 1962. A year later the Tally-Ho opened as the first non-casino hotel on the Strip. Three years later it would be transformed into the Aladdin Hotel and Casino.

Jackie Gaughan started his empire when he bought into the Flamingo Hotel in 1951, following a stint in the military. His next endeavors included the 1963 purchase of the El Cortez Hotel and Casino and other properties in downtown Las Vegas.

On September 28, 1963, President John F. Kennedy became the third President to visit Las Vegas since President Franklin D. Roosevelt dedicated Boulder Dam (Hoover Dam) in 1935. Former President Dwight D. Eisenhower visited Las Vegas on a campaign tour to Hoover Dam in 1952, and former President Harry S. Truman was in town in 1962 to address an American Legion convention. Kennedy arrived at McCarran International Airport and rode in an open limousine to the Las Vegas Convention Center where he spoke to a cheering crowd of 7,500. The saddest day for Las Vegas in the 1960s was November 25, 1963—the day of President Kennedy's funeral. On the day of President Kennedy's assassination, gambling continued at the tables, but the showrooms closed. All casino action in Las Vegas casinos ceased for four hours during Kennedy's funeral. According to news reports, it was the third time in history the casinos had closed. The first closure occurred in the early 1940s in observance of Good Friday at the height of World War II. The second came during four hours following the death of President Franklin D. Roosevelt in 1945. Since 1963, President Bill Clinton, a frequent visitor to Las Vegas, spoke at the Convention Center in 1992, and in the same year, President Jimmy Carter addressed a group of Las Vegans at the Convention Center.

In 1963 Barbra Streisand played to her first Las Vegas audience as a special guest of Liberace at the Riviera Hotel, and the Newton Brothers, Wayne and Jerry, reigned supreme as the top talent attraction in the downtown area. Also in 1963, Joe Well's Thunderbird Downs, a 3/8-mile horse-racing track, opened on the property behind the Thunderbird Hotel and Casino.

Fourteen days before 1963 drew to a close, "Casino de Paris" opened at Dunes Hotel. It was the Dunes' answer to the popular "Lido de Paris" and "Folies Bergere" review shows at the Stardust and Tropicana Hotels, respectively.

TV's favorite talk-show host, Johnny Carson, made his Las Vegas debut at the Sahara Hotel in 1964. That same year, the Beatles made a one-time visit to Las Vegas with a two-concert engagement at the Las Vegas Convention Center.

The Mint Hotel and Casino opened in 1965 in Las Vegas' Casino Center with twenty-six stories and three hundred rooms. Three major hotel-casinos opened in Las Vegas during 1966. The Aladdin Hotel and Casino and Caesars Palace Hotel and Casino opened on the Strip. Caesars Palace would go on to become the best-known casino-resort in the world. The Four Queens Hotel and Casino also opened, on Fremont Street in the downtown area.

During the 1950s virtually all the casinos in Las Vegas were controlled by the mob. A U.S. Senate investigation into criminal activity in the casino industry found that skimming (retaining a portion of the profits) was rife, resulting in tax evasion on stakes and profits.

When legislation allowing corporations to own Las Vegas casinos came into being in 1965, entrepreneur and multimillionaire Howard Hughes was the first to take advantage of the law. When other large corporations followed suit, the finances of the mob proved to be no match for the might of major corporations, and gradually the casino industry was cleaned up.

Two days after Caesars Palace opened in 1966, Latin music king Xavier Cugat and Spanish singer Charo were the first couple to exchange vows at the resort. Cugat had discovered Charo two years earlier in Spain while she was playing a small role in a local production of "Night of the Iguana." He learned later that in addition to her obvious magnetism, she could sing, dance, and play the guitar exquisitely.

In 1966, a new legend arrived in town—Howard Hughes! Hughes and his corporation (Summa Corp.) ushered in the modern era in gambling. He brought in the corporate attitude – and kicked out the good ole' boys – that today is the standard in the industry. The reclusive multimillionaire sneaked into Las Vegas on a special train on Thanksgiving Day 1966, and quickly used the $546 million he reaped from the sale of Trans World Airlines (TWA) to become the state's biggest casino owner. In 1967 Hughes paid Moe Dalitz $13.2 million for the Desert Inn Hotel, in part because the reclusive multimillionaire didn't want to leave the ninth floor of the hotel where he was staying. He eventually acquired five additional hotels and casinos: Sands Hotel, Frontier Hotel, Castaways Hotel, Landmark Hotel, Silver Slipper Gambling Hall, and the land on which the El Rancho Vegas Hotel once stood. He also bought a television station so that he could watch his favorite movies.

Las Vegas' most celebrated wedding of the 1960s took place in 1967 at the Aladdin Hotel with the union of rock 'n 'roll singer Elvis Presley and Priscilla Beaulieu. The same year the Riviera Hotel pulled an entertainment coup by showcasing major stars in its twice-nightly presentation of "Hello Dolly."

The Circus Circus Casino opened in 1968 across from the Riviera Hotel on the Strip. Four years later a four hundred-room hotel was added to the facility.

Two major hotel-casinos opened on Paradise Road, located a block off the Las Vegas Strip, in 1969. The Landmark Hotel and Casino opened eight years after groundbreaking, under the ownership of Howard Hughes. Danny Thomas lit up the hotel's marquee. Kirk Kerkorian's International Hotel and Casino opened next door to the Las Vegas Convention Center. Barbra Streisand kicked off the hotel's talent parade.

Some of the entertainers who were popular in Las Vegas during the 1960s were: All of the Rat Pack, Barbra Streisand, Juliet Prowse, Red Skelton, Connie Francis, Danny Thomas, Smothers Brothers, Liberace, Carol Burnett, Elvis Presley, Andy Williams, Johnny Carson, Wayne Newton, Harry Belafonte, Ann-Margaret, Bob Newhart, Steve Lawrence, Eydie Gorme, Lesley Uggams, the McGuire sisters, The Supremes, Nancy Sinatra, Eleanor Powell, Marlene Dietrich, Louis Armstrong, Jayne Mansfield, Phyllis Diller, Steve Allen, George Gobel, Sid Caesar, Jimmy Durante, Jackie Mason, Woody Allen, Della Reese, Ethel Merman, Kathryn Grayson, Tom Jones, Aretha Franklin, Sarah Vaughan, Mitzi Gaynor, Frank Gorshin, and Richard Pryor.

The following hotels and casinos opened during the 1960s on or near Fremont Street in downtown Las Vegas: This area is now called Casino Center.

Club Bingo, 1962
Lucky Casino, 1963
Lady Luck Casino, 1964
Four Queens Hotel and Casino, 1966

Jerry's Nugget Casino and the Silver Nugget Casino opened in 1964 on North Las Vegas Boulevard. The Silver Dollar Saloon opened the same year at 2501 East Charleston Boulevard.

The following hotels and casinos opened on the Strip during the 1960s:

Flamingo Capri Motel and Casino, 1960
Castaways Hotel and Casino, 1963
Aladdin Hotel and Casino, 1966
Caesars Palace Hotel and Casino, 1966
Frontier Hotel and Casino, 1967
Bonanza Hotel and Casino, 1967
Westward-Ho Hotel and Casino, 1967
Circus Circus Casino, 1968

The Landmark Hotel and Casino and the International Hotel and Casino opened a short distance from the Las Vegas Strip in 1969.

Street View of the Strip, Las Vegas

Fabulous Strip. The Las Vegas Strip is the number one gambling and entertainment center of the world. During the 1920s and 1930s one could hunt jackrabbits anywhere. In the 1960s the Strip stretched from the Sahara Hotel and Casino to the Hacienda Hotel and Casino (now the Mandalay Bay Hotel and Casino). Lili St. Cyr was performing at the Aladdin Hotel when this photograph was taken. Circa 1967, $3-5.

Looking North Along the Las Vegas Strip. From the top of Dunes Hotel, the Flamingo and Sands hotels can be seen on the right while Caesars Palace and Frontier hotels are on the left. At the center right are the Landmark and International hotels. The Flamingo Hotel's erupting flower pylon sign was erected in 1968. Circa 1969, $3-5.

The Strip, Nighttime View. The Las Vegas Strip at night is Broadway, Coney Island, and the World's Fair all rolled in one, a carnival that swings in quick tempo in each of the luxurious resort hotel-casinos until the wee hours of the morning. The pace is just as fast and the lights even brighter in the casino area in downtown Las Vegas. Circa 1967, $1-3.

Looking North on the Las Vegas Strip. Shown on the left side of the Strip are Dunes Hotel, Caesars Palace, Castaways Hotel, Frontier Hotel, Stardust Hotel, and the Circus Circus Casino. On the right are the Bonanza, Flamingo, Sands, Desert Inn, Riviera, and Sahara hotels. The two buildings in the top right corner are the Landmark and International hotels. Circa 1970s, $7-9.

Looking East on Fremont Street, Downtown Las Vegas. The two tallest buildings are the 26-story Mint Hotel and Casino and the fifteen-story Fremont Hotel and Casino. Downtown Las Vegas was often referred to as "Glitter Gulch" and "Casino Center." Circa 1965, $3-5.

Daytime view of "Glitter Gulch." Looking East towards the gambling center of downtown Las Vegas. Circa 1960s, $3-5.

Close-up View. This is the brightest intersection in the world. The Golden Nugget, Mint, Binion's Horseshoe, Fremont, and Four Queens made this nighttime view look like daytime. Circa 1968, $7-9.

Howard Hughes. As a young movie producer in the 1940s and 1950s, Howard Hughes loved to come to Las Vegas. The small gambling town offered an escape from Hollywood, and Hughes loved excitement, gambling, and beautiful women. Las Vegas' ambiance made it a perfect place and in the 1960s, flush with $546.5 million from his sale of Trans World Airlines, Hughes set out to buy Las Vegas, casino by casino. The Howard Hughes' Las Vegas era began in the pre-dawn hours of November 27, 1966, when he arrived, unannounced, via his private train. His entourage rented the top floor of the Desert Inn Hotel and Casino. When told he would have to leave to make way for coveted high-rollers coming in for New Year's Eve, Hughes resolved the problem by buying the Desert Inn. It started a buying spree that included the Frontier, Sands, Castaways, and Landmark hotels and casinos, and the Silver Slipper Gambling Hall. Hughes also bought up nearly every piece of vacant land on the Strip and thousands of acres on the northwest side of Las Vegas. The emergence of Hughes also marked the beginning of the end of mob influence over Las Vegas' casino industry. Hughes left Las Vegas four years after his mysterious arrival; however, his imprint remains today. Circa 1960s, $5-7.

Popular Location for Weddings. Circa 1960s, $3-5. Las Vegas has dozens of wedding chapels, including the Little Chapel in the West, some open twenty-four hours; others featuring more than one chapel for simultaneous ceremonies. Many of the hotels either had facilities or could easily arrange weddings. The roll call of celebrity marriages in Las Vegas is a long one. The "A" list of 1950s and 1960s weddings included:

1953: Rita Hayworth and Dick Haymes, September 24

1955: Joan Crawford and Alfred Steele, May 10, Flamingo Hotel

1957: Bing Crosby and Catherine Grant, October 24; Steve Lawrence and Eydie Gorme, December 29, El Rancho Vegas;

1958: Joanne Woodward and Paul Newman, January 1; David and Ellie Janssen, August 23, 1958, El Rancho Vegas

1960: Nancy Sinatra and Tommy Sands, September 11, Sands Hotel

1962: Mary Tyler Moore and Grant Tinker, June 1, Dunes Hotel

1963: Allen Ludden and Betty White, June 14; Vic Damone and Judy Rawlins, October 24, Sands Hotel

1965: Jane Fonda and Roger Vadim, August 14; Judy Garland and Mark Herron, November 13, Sands Hotel

1966: Brigitt Bardot and Gunter Sachs, July 13

1967: Elvis Presley and Pricilla Beaulieu, May 1, Aladdin Hotel; Ann-Margret and Roger Smith, May 8, Riviera Hotel; Leslie Ann Warren and Jon Peters, May 13, Sahara Hotel

1968: Wayne and Elaine Newton, June 1, 1968, Flamingo Hotel

Read All About It! In 1963 *The Green Felt Jungle* was published, a book-length expose of Las Vegas that claimed to "blast the lid off the fabulous entertainment capital of the world and lay bare a corrupt jungle of inequity." The book was co-authored by *Las Vegas Sun* reporter Ed Reid and fellow journalist Ovid Demaris. It became a runaway best seller overnight, turning Las Vegas' "open secret" into a national preoccupation. The book is a shocking, fascinating expose of Las Vegas. The corruption detailed is almost unbelievable. Considering the material in the book, it's surprising that its two ex-newspapermen authors were not buried in the desert surrounding Las Vegas. It described Las Vegas as a cesspool of crime fed by organized gambling. Shown are two paperback editions of the original book published by Trident Press in 1963. Circa 1964, $15-20.

Memorabilia. Gaming chips from Las Vegas casinos that opened during the 1960s. Circa 1960s, $3-40.

Popular Clubs of the 1960s

Aladdin Hotel and Casino

Edmond Lowe, of Lowes Theater Chain, built the Tallyho in 1963. It was the first major Strip hotel without a casino. It didn't work. In 1964 a new group bought the hotel, renamed it Kings Crown, and began a $15 million expansion project, which included a showroom, new façade, and casino. However, the new owners were denied a gambling license and Kings Crown never opened. Along came an entrepreneur who turned the hotel into a major Strip hotel-casino.

Milton Prell, the former owner and operator of the Sahara Hotel and Casino, paid $19 million for Kings Crown in the fall of 1965. He began immediate renovation, which included a new 500-seat showroom (Baghdad Theater), a large casino, a lounge, a 150-seat gourmet restaurant, an Olympic-size swimming pool, a 7,500 capacity theater geared to special events, and an 18-hole Par-3 golf course.

Aladdin Hotel and Casino opened at 3667 Las Vegas Boulevard April 1, 1966. It was the first major hotel-casino to open on the Las Vegas Strip since Stardust Hotel opened in 1958. The Aladdin's Magic lamp sign, built by the Young Electric Sign Company (YESCO), rose fifteen stories, cost $750,000, and used over 40,000 light bulbs.

Prell introduced an innovative main showroom policy by offering three completely different shows twice nightly, beginning at 8 p.m. and ending at 6 a.m., with no cover or minimum charge. Jackie Mason, noted TV comic, was the first headliner at the Aladdin. Following the Jackie Mason Show was the Jet Set Review and a musical-comedy show that featured the Three Cheers vocal and the Petite Rockette Dancers. Later stars appearing at the Aladdin were Frankie Valli, Cheech & Chong, Jackie Gayle, Rusty Warren, Redd Foxx, and Jackie Vernon.

Milton Prell was a personal friend of Elvis Presley. The most celebrated wedding of the 1960s was staged at the Aladdin in May 1967. Priscilla Beaulieu and the King were married in Prell's private suite. Prell suffered a heart attack not long after the wedding, and the glamour times of the Aladdin started to fade. The hotel was sold in 1968, business continued to decline, and sold again to St. Louis businessman Peter Webbe. It was sold again in 1972 to Richard Daily for $5 million. Even after a $50 million expansion in 1976 added a twenty-story high-rise tower and a 20,000-seat theater, the hotel continued to have problems. In 1979, the Nevada Gaming

Control Board closed the Aladdin for its underworld connections. It had been referred to as the "R & R center for the underworld."

Wayne Newton and Ed Torres reopened the Aladdin in 1980, ran it for a while; then after the partnership failed, Newton sold his interests in the hotel. Further legal and financial troubles plagued the hotel and the Aladdin entered bankruptcy in 1984. In 1985 Asian millionaire Ginja Yasuda bought the hotel for approximately $52 million, and the Aladdin Hotel limped along, managed by a bankruptcy court trustee.

The 32-year-old Aladdin Hotel and Casino was imploded April 27, 1998 at approximately 7:30 p.m. to an estimated crowd of 20,000 onlookers. Preparation of the implosion took one month and cost $2 million. The building went from standing to rubble in less than twenty seconds. A very impressive sight! Future plans for the property was to build a new Aladdin resort.

On August 17, 2000 a new Arabian-themed Aladdin Hotel and the Desert Passage Shopping Center opened. Nadel Architects designed it with interior décor from Brennan Beer Gorman Monk. The new Aladdin resort cost $1.4 billion and had a 2,567-room hotel. The new Aladdin resort had twenty-one restaurants, a 135,000-square-foot casino containing 2,500 slot machines and ninety-eight table games, two outdoor swimming pools, 75,000-square-feet of meeting rooms, a 7,000 seat theater for the Performing Arts and the London Club, and a 35,000 square-foot European style luxury gaming salon. The Aladdin resort had financial problems and filed for bankruptcy in 2002.

In 2003 Planet Hollywood and Starwood Hotels & Resorts bought the Aladdin resort for $635 million. On September 1, 2004 the Aladdin Hotel became the Planet Hollywood Hotel and Casino.

Aladdin Hotel and Casino. After nine years of no new hotels, Las Vegas welcomed Aladdin Hotel and Casino April 1, 1966, named for the owner of a magic lamp in "Arabian Nights" legend. Circa 1966, $6-8.

Tallyho Hotel. In 1963, the Tallyho opened as a non-gambling hotel on the Strip. It went bankrupt in two years when the Kings Crown Casino was added but denied a gambling license. Milton Prell bought the Tallyho in 1965 and built his Aladdin Hotel around it. Circa 1965, $5-7.

Greetings from Las Vegas. The Aladdin Hotel and Casino had one of the most attractive hotel fronts in Las Vegas. The fifteen-story magic lamp sign cost $750,000 and used over 40,000 light bulbs. It incorporated hints of jewelry, veils, magic lamps, and fantasy. Circa 1966, $6-8.

The Magical Lamp. After the Aladdin lamp was removed from the old Aladdin Hotel sign, it sat in the sign graveyard at Young Electric Sign Company (YESCO) for some time. It was later installed in the Neon Museum in downtown Las Vegas. *Author photograph*.

Advertising Card. Large postcard advertising the "Vive Paris Viva" entertainment show appearing in the Baghdad Theater at the Aladdin Hotel and Casino. Circa 1960s, $6-8.

Memorabilia, Aladdin Hotel and Casino. Playing cards ($4-6), $5 gaming chip ($10-30), $1 gaming chip ($3-5), matchbook ($8-12), keno playing booklet ($3-5), keno form ($1-3), swizzle stick ($2-4), pen ($1-3), magnet ($1-3), and keno booklet ($2-4). Circa 1960s.

Bonanza Hotel and Casino

The 160-room Bonanza Hotel and Casino opened July 1, 1967 at the corner of Las Vegas Boulevard South and Flamingo Road. Larry Wolf, a New York attorney, built it.

The Bonanza Hotel was furnished in early 1900s décor. When you entered the Bonanza you might have thought you were on the set of a western movie. It was like a page out of the Old West. The theme, décor, and dress of the employees were western. Every effort was made to recreate an authentic western atmosphere.

The Bonanza was located across from Dunes Hotel and Casino, and had all the facilities associated with Las Vegas resort hotels: swimming pool, casino, 24-hour Chuck Wagon, several bars, a main showroom called the Opera House, a swinging lounge named the Corral, nearly 200-rooms, a wide screen "Movie Palace" with 411 plush-back seats, and a gourmet dining room called the Cattlemen's Restaurant.

The 500-seat Opera House featured not only western productions but popular entertainers as well, such as Sarah Vaughn, Dale Robertson, and Marty Robbins. It was a spacious room, with three tiers and a balcony affording an excellent view of the stage from any table. Food was not served during performances and there was a $4.50 minimum for three drinks for either the early (8 p.m.) or late (midnight) show. Drinks were served by lovely Indian maidens that were exquisitely attired in alluring micro-mini "buckskins."

If you were a fan of musical groups such as Wolfman Jack, the Olympics, the Kirby Stone Company, and the Swingin' Lads, then you felt right at home at the Bonanza's 200-seat Corral Lounge. The Corral was a popular late-night spot on the Strip, featuring continuous entertainment from 9 p.m. till 5 a.m. There were often several celebrities who were appearing at other shows in the audience.

The Bonanza's Chuck Wagon was located in the Ponderosa Room. From 2 a.m. until 11 a.m. in the morning the breakfast buffet cost 99¢. And from 11 a.m. until 2 a.m. the full dinner buffet was $1.69. It was a tremendous value and a beautiful feast. Around the walls of Ponderosa's coffee shop were framed photographs of the great cowboy stars of the movies including Gene Autry and Tom Mix.

After Kirk Kerkorian bought the Bonanza Hotel in 1970 he demolished it to make room for the new MGM Grand Hotel and Casino he was going to build.

Howdy from Las Vegas. The Bonanza Hotel and Casino has all the facilities associated with the fine Las Vegas resort hotels: gourmet restaurant; swimming pool; 24-hour Chuck Wagon; several bars; a main showroom called the Opera House; a swinging lounge named the Corral; 160 rooms; and a wide screen "Movie Palace" with 411 plush-back seats. The Bonanza's Opera House seated 500 guests and featured popular entertainers such as Dale Robertson, Sarah Vaughn, and Marty Robbins. Circa 1967, $7-9.

Caesars Palace Hotel and Casino

Las Vegas' first empire opened August 5, 1966. It was the largest and most expensive hotel-casino ever to be put up in one piece. Adjacent to the Dunes Hotel and across from the Flamingo Hotel, at 3570 Las Vegas Boulevard South, it was called Caesars Palace Resort Hotel and Casino. It was an "Americanized" version of the splendors of Ancient Greece and Rome. It cost $25 million to build, a grand sum in 1965-66 dollars. Caesars was originally planned to be named "Desert Palace."

When founder Jay Sarno began designing his fantasy resort, Caesars Palace, in 1963, he rejected the "cowboy look" popular with other hotel-casinos in the area. Instead, he tried to create "something romantic, yet... cognizant of the sun and desert area." After spending a year on the design with the help of an architect and an interior designer, the plans for a modern resort based on ancient, classical lines was complete. This completely different approach to a hotel-casino immediately established Caesars as the most luxurious facility in Las Vegas and the most famous casino name in the world. Julius would have been proud.

The opening celebration cost an astronomical $1 million and lasted three days, as 1,800 invited guests and celebrities dined on two tons of filet mignon and quaffed 50,000 glasses of champagne.

Andy Williams, one of the top singers and TV stars of the day, performed in the Circus Maximus showroom. Two days later, Latin musician Xavier Cugat and salsa dancer Charo became the first couple to marry on the premises.

Casino hosts Johnny (Tarzan) Weismueller and heavyweight champion Joe Louis greeted customers. Weismueller used to run through the casino screaming his famous Tarzan call.

The original facility was comprised of 680 guest rooms in a crescent-shaped, fourteen-story tower; the Roman Forum Casino; the 800-seat Circus Maximus showroom, and two restaurants, the Garden of the Gods pool complex, and the 25,000-square-foot Coliseum Convention complex. Beautiful hand-carved woods and Italian marble—taken from the same quarry in Carrara, Italy that provided Michelangelo with his fine sculpting material—graced the floors, walls, and ceilings. Fountains, statues, and gardens are found throughout the hotel grounds. One of the largest sculptures is a twenty-foot replica of Michelangelo's masterpiece, David, which weighed more than nine tons and took longer than ten months to complete. The entire complex covers thirty-four acres with sixteen acres of landscaping and parking facilities for 1,200 automobiles.

Caesars Palace. On August 5, 1966, Jay Sarno's Caesars Palace opened on the Strip—the resort raised the bar for elegance. The grand Romanesque resort occupied thirty-four acres. It was the newest, most magnificent resort in the fun capital of the world, with top star entertainment, lavish cuisine, and 700 palatial guest rooms and suites. Andy Williams headlined the three-day-long opening gala at Caesars Palace. Sarno reportedly dropped the possessive apostrophe in "Caesar's" as a way of conveying to guests that the hotel belonged not to a single Caesar but to anyone who wanted to live like a Roman emperor for a few days. Circa 1966, $5-7.

Imported Italian Cypress trees lined the entrance roadway. To either side of the massive front doorways were additional marble statues imported from Italy at a cost of $200,000.

Caesars Palace has the most luxurious and unique chandelier that ever graced a Nevada hotel. Costing $125,000 and containing more than 100,000 crystals, it is the world's largest chandelier measuring 96' x 66' feet across.

The five-acre Garden of the Gods pool complex maintained the ambience of the ancient world. Designed after the Pompeii Baths of Rome, the sweeping lawns and graceful trees served as a perfect setting for the Olympic size swimming pool that was tiled with 8,000 individually shaped and hand-mounted pieces of marble from the Carrara quarry.

By the end of its first month of operation, Caesars Palace was raking in cash at a phenomenal rate. The money was pouring in so fast that instead of counting the cash after each shift, employees would simply separate it by denomination and weigh it. A million dollars in $100 bills weighed a little over twenty pounds.

The Circus Maximus showroom has been noted for years for its name entertainment. Opening night headliner was Andy Williams, and the list of celebrities who have performed there since reads like a list of who's who: Bill Cosby, Frank Sinatra, Julie Andrews, Shirley MacLaine, Woody Allen, Jack Benny, Ed Sullivan, Gene Kelly, Bob Cummings, Harry Belafonte, Merle Haggard, Willie Nelson, Julio Iglasias, Johnny Mathis, Joey Heatherton, Lena Horne, Liberace, Jackie Gleason, Loretta Swit, Diana Ross, Joan Rivers, Paul Anka, Aretha Franklin, Carol Channing, Ann-Margaret, Tony Bennett, Sammy Davis, Jr., Richard Pryor, David Copperfield, Tom Jones, George Burns, Jerry Seinfeld, Dolly Parton, Luciano Pavaroti, and on and on.

Evel Knievel, a 29-year-old daredevil who was barnstorming America leaping over cars and buses with a motorcycle, had a crazy idea about jumping over the 25-foot-tall water fountain in front of Caesars Palace. The executives at the resort liked the idea.

Knievel erected a special ramp that would guide his motorcycle over the fountain, placing him on a wider ramp for landing. In theory, it would work. In reality, it failed.

On New Year's Eve 1967, Evel flew 150-feet in the air and landed on the edge of the ramp, causing both the bike and rider to career crazily into a cement retaining wall. Knievel spent months in a local hospital. After the failed jump Evel became the biggest name in motorcycle stunts.

On April 14, 1989, Robbie Knievel, son of the first man to ever try a leap over the Caesar Palace fountain, accomplished what his father was not able to do—land successfully. Robbie, like his father, went on to gain fame as one of the great motorcycle stuntmen in the world.

With beauty and grandeur visible wherever you look, it's not surprising that Caesars Palace became a favorite location for Hollywood film productions. The first film to be made at Caesars was the 1968 movie "Where It's At," starring David Janssen, Don Rickles, and Brenda Vaccaro. Warren Beatty and Elizabeth Taylor filmed "The Only Game in Town" there in 1969. "The Gambler," starring James Caan, Mel Brook's "History of the World-Part I," "Oh, God! You Devil," and "Rainman," with Tom Cruise and Dustin Hoffman were also filmed at Caesars.

In 1969, Sarno and his partners, Jimmy Hoffa's Teamsters' Pension Fund, sold Caesars Palace for $60 million to Lum's Corporation, which owned a chain of 440 restaurants around the country that specialized in selling hot dogs steamed in beer.

Over the years, with several different owners, several high-rise hotel room towers, additional casinos, restaurants, and a parking structure were added to Caesars. In May 1992, a new 875,000-square-foot shopping extravaganza, the Forum at Caesars, with gondolas plying artificial lakes, opened with ninety stores, at a total cost of $100 million.

Beginning in 1979, Caesars Palace was the site of many of the most celebrated fights of all time including the Holmes-Ali bout of 1980 that ended Ali's career; Leonard vs. Hearns in 1981, the largest grossing fight in boxing history; and "The Fight" of 1985 between Hagler and Hearns that earned Hagler the reputation of boxing's best. Caesars became the world's boxing capital.

Caesars Palace now has three casinos — the Roman Forum Casino, the Palace Court Casino, and the Olympic Casino — that have everything from blackjack to keno, baccarat and roulette to craps and pai gow—and over 2,000 slot machines. Located in the Olympic Casino is a massive Race and Sports Book. Caesars also has 3,340 rooms spread out over five towers: Augustus, Centurion, Forum, Palace, and Roman.

The history of Caesars Palace is epic; its luxuries are legendary and its headliners were some of the most dazzling stars on the planet. Jay Sarno, even in his wildest dreams, couldn't have imagined the empire it has become today.

Caesars Palace has been a Las Vegas Strip champion since it opened in 1966. Even today, surrounded by billion dollar megaresorts, including the Bellagio, Mandalay Bay, Venetian, MGM Grand, and Winn Las Vegas, Caesars is still a larger-than-life resort.

Sculptured Entrance. The statuary collection at Caesars Palace was specially sculptured in Carrara, Italy by Europe's foremost masters. Visitors walked past several statues and fountains to enter the resort. Circa 1960s, $5-7.

Entrance, Caesers Palace. This view of Caesars Palace shows its columns and long, tree-lined entrance. On December 31, 1967, daredevil cyclist Evel Knievel closed out the year, and nearly his life, when he jumped a record 144 feet over the Roman fountains in front of 10,000 spectators. Evel was not successful on his landing. However he was on hand twenty-two years later to watch along with 50,000 excited fans at the hotel and a national television audience as his daredevil son Robbie carried out the jump flawlessly. Circa 1960s, $3-5.

A Roman-Grecian Fantasyland. When Caesars Palace opened, Julius wasn't there, but all the magnificence of this Roman-Grecian fantasyland would have awed even him. From the imported marble statuary, to the costumed "goddesses" cocktail servers, and the world famous entertainers, Caesars caught the attention of the world. Jay Sarno's Caesars Palace took lavish casino theming to an entirely new level. It quickly became one of the world's most famous casinos, and one that certain gambling-obsessed Roman emperors would have been glad to visit. Cancelled 1969, $5-7.

Roulette, Caesars Palace Hotel and Casino. Circa 1960s, $6-8.

Memorabilia, Caesars Palace Hotel and Casino. Playing cards ($4-6), $5 baccarat chip ($10-20), Roulette chip ($2-4), $5 gaming chip ($8-20), $1 gaming chip ($3-5), matchbook ($2-8), shampoo ($1-3), keno guide ($2-4), keno form ($1-3), swizzle stick ($1-3), and pen ($1-3). Circa 1960s.

Castaways Hotel and Casino

Castaways Hotel and Casino opened in 1957 as the San Souci Hotel at 3320 Las Vegas Boulevard South (the Strip). The name was changed September 1, 1963 by a group of investors headed by Ike P. LaRue, who remodeled it. It consisted of a casino, a showroom, a restaurant, two wings of hotel rooms, and a lounge. At the time, Castaways Casino had nine table games, one keno lounge, and 152 slot machines. The lounge had a 1,500-gallon fish tank behind the bar; however, the tank didn't have any fish in it. A nude showgirl swam lazily through the water three times a day holding her breath while wide-eyed patrons held theirs.

In 1964, Breck Wall's "Bottoms Up" show debuted in Castaways' showroom and ran for eighteen weeks. Other delightful, but silly shows of the times included "Watusi Scandals," "Around The World A Go-Go," and "Holiday In The Orient."

Lord Buckley was a popular comedian in the 1960s, and the Castaways showroom is where he made it big. Red Foxx, the most famous person to appear at Castaways, made his Las Vegas debut in October 1963.

Castaways experienced several periods of financial difficulties, but while open, was always an innovative place. For example, one of the biggest events in Las Vegas today is the boxing matches—it all started at Castaways with the "Strip Fight of the Week." And while today just about every casino has a sports book, it was Castaways that rocked the industry when they introduced a $100,000 football handicap in 1978. During the hard times in Las Vegas, while many casinos were looking at Canada, the Orient, and Europe for players, Castaways simply told residents of Las Vegas that they were welcome.

In 1971, Howard Hughes' Summa Corporation bought Castaways for $3 million, remodeled, and even made the place home to radio station KVEG. Castaways survived primarily by smiling more and always welcoming local gamblers. In 1972, Castaways' showroom featured the "Tom Jones Show," which featured a number of lusty ballads and a chorus line of footlight gals dressed in bosom-flashing Elizabethan costumes.

Castaways Hotel and Casino closed July 19, 1987. The famous casino disappeared shortly thereafter as a bulldozer scraped it away to make room for the Mirage Hotel and Casino.

Greetings from Las Vegas

Castaways Hotel. It had 230 rooms, an Olympic-sized swimming pool, and a 24-hour casino and restaurant. It also had a fourteen-ton teakwood "Gateway to Luck" replica of an East Indian temple located on the hotel grounds. In the summer of 1964 Redd Foxx entertained at the Castaways Hotel. Circa 1960s, $8-10.

Castaways Hotel and Casino. Located at 3360 Las Vegas Boulevard South, the former site of San Souci Hotel and Casino, Castaways was noted for its intimate charm and friendliness. Howard Hughes reportedly bought Castaways Hotel and Casino across from Sands Hotel and Casino because of the land underneath. Stretching from the northernmost border of Caesars Palace all the way to the end of a very long block, the plot was slated to be the site of Sands Hotel West, an enormous resort city that Hughes planned one day to build. Circa 1960s, $4-6.

Memorabilia, Castaways Hotel and Casino. Playing cards ($4-7), $1 gaming chip ($6-75), $5,000 fantasy chip ($2-4), matchbook ($10-12), and swizzle stick ($2-4). Circa 1960s.

Circus Circus Casino

Designed as the world's largest combined casino and amusement center, the $15 million Circus Circus was Las Vegas' first family-style gambling facility. It was built by hotelman Jay Sarno, who built Caesars Palace, and opened October 18, 1968, across from the Riviera Hotel and Casino, at 2880 Las Vegas Boulevard South (the Strip). Circus Circus Casino was the largest permanently based circus in the world.

On opening night herds of people were waiting to get in the casino. The first circus act was the Flying Palacinis. Ringmaster Clarence Hoffman, a dead ringer for Albert Einstein, welcomed guests by saying, "Ladies and Gentlemen. Introducing Circus Circus, the most exciting casino in the world!" The circus acts were scheduled to perform from 8 p.m. to 2 a.m., however, the excitement lasted until 6 a.m., when the acts finally had to stop due to fatigue. But the most striking event of the evening was the graceful body of a trapeze artist swinging through the air overhead, sixty feet above the casino floor and in full view of the gamblers below. The sounds of slot machines and the drone of the dealers mixed with the squeals of laughter from children who gazed mystified at the acrobats, clowns, and jugglers around them.

The pink and white striped structure was constructed in the form of a giant big top and contained fun outlets that would appeal to kids from ages eight to eighty. The casino area, slightly longer than a football field, was located on the ground floor. Midway-type games were located on the mezzanine, which completely encircled the gambling area. Sarno's innovative concept was to encourage parents to bring the children with them. Now Las Vegas had a casino with elephants, trained dogs, shooting gallery, unicyclists, trapeze performers, jugglers, acrobats, popcorn, peanuts, and fifteen clowns. Free circus performances were presented continuously throughout the day and evening, however, there was a $1 admission fee to get in the casino.

Five statues were created by renowned artist Montyne and installed at the Circus Circus Casino. These circus themed statues remained by the casino's main marquee for the next thirty-eight years. In 2006 four of the statues – the female acrobat; Gargantua, the gorilla; the lion; and the Balancer – were destroyed and only the Clown remained.

Taking photographs in a casino in the 1960s was a no-no. One time at the Circus Circus Casino, this author hid his camera inside an empty paper popcorn bag and walked through the casino taking pictures. He got away with this "crime" and now has several of these photographs in his photo file. The popcorn bag did not look out of place in this casino.

Hundreds of acts appeared at Circus Circus Casino over the years and run the gamut from jugglers to dog acts, clowns to high-wire artists. But the most exciting acts were the trapeze artists. One such group was the Flying Cavarettas, consisting of family members Maureen, Terry, Jimmy, and Kandy Cavaretta, all accomplished professionals.

Once a gambler in the Circus Circus Casino looked up at the high wire overhead to see one of the flying Cavarettas flip over three times in the air and land in the arms of her brother. The act distracted him just long enough for the dice shooter to roll a crap three, wiping out his winnings. He then collected his remaining gaming chips, glared at a cavorting clown, shouldered past a lady stilt walker, and stalked out of the casino to go across the Strip to the Riviera to see if Lady Luck was on his side over there.

Circus Circus struggled for several years. In 1972, Circus Circus became a full-fledged resort when it added a 400-room hotel tower. In 1974 Sarno sold the resort to William Bennett, an Arizona businessman, and Del Webb, and within a year a fifteen-story, 395-room tower was added, which brought the number of rooms at the resort to 795.

In 1976 the "Lucky the Clown" sign was added to the facility. Designed and built by Young Electric Sign Company (YESCO), the huge beaming figure, rendered in red, yellow, orange, and white paint and neon, points gaily into the casino. This imposing display sign weighed 84-tons, was seventy-eight feet wide, twelve feet thick, and 123-feet high. The sign had a marquee display board, measuring 41' x 50' feet, which was cleverly incorporated into the design. Also, the sign has 1,232 fluorescent lamps, 14,498 incandescent bulbs, and three-quarters of a mile of neon tubing, all connected by 100,000 feet of electrical wiring.

Additional hotel rooms were added to the Circus Circus Hotel and Casino. In 1980, five three-story motel buildings were added. In 1986, a 29-story Skyrise Tower, the gaming area was enlarged to over 100,000-square-feet; new dining areas, bars, and other modifications were also made to the resort.

Circus Circus has added a five-acre theme park called Grand Slam Canyon at the rear of the hotel/casino. The park is a takeoff of the Grand Canyon, with 140-foot peaks, a ninety-foot Havasupai Falls, and a coursing river. The entire scenic park, covered by a space-frame dome, provides Grand Slam Canyon with complete climate control.

Circus Circus Enterprises, Inc., a public corporation, became the most profitable hotel-casino organization in the world. In addition to Circus Circus, Slots A Fun, and Silver City Casino in Las Vegas, the Circus' empire had a sister hotel in Reno, two hotel-casinos in Laughlin, the 4,032-room Excalibur, and the plus pyramid-shaped Luxor Hotel and Casino in Las Vegas that opened in 1993. The Circus Circus organization was later named the Mandalay Resort Group after the company's popular tropical-themed property on the south end of the Strip.

The Circus Circus Casino. It opened on the Strip October 18, 1968 for kids from ages 8 to 80. The "Big Top" required over 50 thousand gallons of hot-pink and white paint to dress the more than 3,000 yards of concrete (enough to build 250 average sized homes) and enclosed not only a gambling casino, but also a permanent circus show with trapeze acts, clowns, and high-wire performers; fourteen different restaurants and bars; and a Midway consisting of numerous games of skill and chance. In the center of the "Big Top's" main floor was the gaming area. The circus acts performed directly above the center pit gaming area, so patrons could watch performers from the casino area between wagers or from the mezzanine area. Even the hundreds of slot machines are unusual. When a jackpot is hit, they play tunes, ring bells, and flash multi-colored lights. The casino employees are garbed in circus-type costumes. One of the more unusual aspects of the Circus Circus Casino is that it's suitable for the entire family, with games of all types to play. It was Las Vegas' first theme casino for families. When it opened, the casino had a $1 admission fee. Circa 1968, $10-12.

Feeling Lucky? These gamblers are hoping to hit it big at the Circus Circus Casino. Shown are players and dealers at blackjack, craps and roulette games. Circa 1960s, $5-7.

Entertainment Palace. The Circus Circus Casino, a $15 million gaming and entertainment palace, was an entirely new concept in show business. It was a permanently built circus that displayed before the public some of the greatest circus performers in the world. Beautiful girls in colorful costumes catered to customers in fourteen bars and eateries. Circa 1968, $6-8.

Slot Machine. Few things symbolize Las Vegas like the slot machine. During the 1940s-1960s the most common coinage used were pennies, nickels, quarters, and silver dollars. Today, many machines accept $100 and $500 tokens and paper input. Shown are rows of slot machines at Circus Circus Casino. It was the only casino in Las Vegas where the customer was serenaded with various types of music when they hit a jackpot. Circa 1960s, $1-3.

Memorabilia, Circus Circus Casino. Playing cards ($4-6), $5 gaming chip ($8-15), $1 gaming chip ($3-50), key holder ($5-7), matchbook ($2-4), napkin ($1-3), and keno form ($1-3). Circa 1960s.

Club Bingo

The Las Vegas Club was located at 23 East Fremont Street in downtown Las Vegas. In 1951 the Las Vegas Club relocated across the street and the Westerner Gambling House occupied this site from 1951 until 1962; it then became Club Bingo, a casino with slot machines and blackjack tables. In 1983, Club Bingo became part of the Pioneer Club, which was located next door.

Flamingo Capri Motel and Casino

The Flamingo Capri Motel was located at 3535 Las Vegas Boulevard South next to the Flamingo Hotel and Casino. In 1971, Ralph Lewis Engelstad, a general contractor, purchased the motel, a longtime landmark with nine acres of land. As his own general contractor, Engelstad built some low-rise buildings on the site and employed a staff of 250. Gaming began at the Flamingo Capri Motel and Casino a year later, in 1972. An arrangement was made with the Flamingo Hotel to provide hotel, room service, and accessibility to all hotel facilities for the motel guests.

By 1974, the motel had 180 air-conditioned rooms and the Shangri-La pool, which featured a two-story waterfall, spa, and poolside bar. Later the motel expanded to 650-rooms.

On November 1, 1979, the name was retired, and the Imperial Palace and Casino opened with 1,100 employees. This Oriental themed hotel became the seventh-largest hotel in the world.

Four Queens Hotel and Casino

Located where the White Cross Drug Store was at 202 East Fremont Street, in downtown Las Vegas, Four Queens Hotel and Casino opened in 1965. It began as a pint-size property with 120 rooms and a 20,000-square-foot casino and grew into a famous Glitter Gulch landmark. Ben Goffstein, who named the facility after his four daughters, founded Four Queens. Goffstein, who had given up the presidency of the Riviera Hotel and Casino to fulfill his dream of the Four Queens, wanted a "class joint" that placed more emphasis on gambling instead of expensive entertainment. The Four Queens had the atmosphere reminiscent of nineteenth century New Orleans.

In 1976, the casino was expanded to 33,000 square feet. Another casino expansion in 1977 enlarged the casino to 40,000 square feet, which now took up the full block of Fremont Street from Casino Center to Third Street.

In 1981, another 8,000-square-foot of casino space and an eighteen-story, 400-room tower were added.

Four Queens is one of the few Las Vegas casinos that invites visitors to take photographs.

The facility had the world's largest slot machine. More than nine feet high and almost twenty feet long, six people could play it at one time! It was the Mother of all giant slot machines.

Four Queens Hotel and Casino. This hotel opened in the heart of downtown Las Vegas in 1965. Circa 1965, $4-6.

World's Largest Slot Machine. The Queens Machine, at the time the world's largest slot machine, was located at Four Queens Hotel and Casino. Six people could play at the same time. Circa 1960s, $2-4.

Memorabilia, Four Queens Hotel and Casino. Playing cards ($4-6), $5 gaming chip ($8-12), $2.50 gaming chip ($6-10), $1 gaming chip ($3-6), 50¢ gaming chip ($3-6), matchbook ($1-4), napkin ($1-3), keno form ($1-3), and pen ($1-3). Circa 1960s.

Frontier Hotel and Casino

The Last Frontier Hotel opened October 30, 1942 at 3120 Las Vegas Boulevard South. It was the second resort to open on the Strip. In 1955 a new, modern hotel-casino, like the others on the Strip, was built on the property and called "New Frontier Hotel and Casino."

It was in the space-age themed New Frontier Hotel, in the Venus Room, in 1956 that 21-year-old Elvis Presley made his Las Vegas debut. He was billed as the "Atomic Powered Singer" and shared the bill with Shecky Greene. Presley was widely written off as a flop, with *Newsweek* calling him a "jug of corn liquor at a champagne party."

The New Frontier Hotel became the Frontier Hotel and Casino in July 1967. A few months later Howard Hughes' Summa Corporation purchased the Frontier Hotel for $14 million. Frontier, one of Hughes' sparkling stars, was a success from the instant its doors opened.

Constructed in the form of a curved horseshoe, Frontier incorporated the most modern innovations in hotel industry, reflected in the decorative appointments and the naming of its many public rooms, dining areas, and convention spaces. Towering palms and evergreen trees against the white columned, bronze glass, and gold marble façade of the building and in the dramatic sunken gardens of its huge center courtyard created an oasis-like setting in the desert surroundings.

It also boasted one of the world's tallest free-standing signs, costing in excess of $1 million and rising about two hundred feet in the air in the hotel entrance. The huge marquee listed the names of entertainers appearing in the Frontier Hotel's showrooms and flashed a red carpet welcome to arriving guests. Some of the entertainers to perform at Frontier during the 1960s and 1970s were Frank Sinatra, Jimmy Durante, Phil Harris, Wayne Newton, Teresa Brewer, Bob Newhart, Flip Wilson, George Carlin, Bobby Darin, Eddie Fisher, Frank Gorshin, and Robert Goulet.

In 1969 the hotel was enlarged. The following year saw the final performance of the legendary Motown group, Diana Ross & the Supremes. In 1980 the Little Church of the West was moved to the Hacienda Hotel and Casino. Siegfried & Roy began their starring roles in the show "Beyond Belief" in 1981. The duo performed 3,500 shows before more than three million onlookers over a seven-year period. In 1990 the 386-room Atrium Tower was constructed giving the Frontier a total of 986 rooms.

In May 2007, Frontier Hotel was sold to El Ad Properties for $1.2 billion who imploded the sixteen-story Atrium Tower in the early morning hours of November 13, 2007. Fireworks and choreographed explosions delighted onlookers who made a special trip to see the dramatic end to the once popular Frontier Hotel and Casino. The 34.5-acre site will be used to build a new Las Vegas megaresort.

Frontier Hotel and Casino. One of Howard Hughes' sparkling stars, the Frontier was a success from the instant it opened in 1967. Constructed in the form of a curved horseshoe, the hotel incorporated the most modern innovations available in the industry, reflected in the decorative appointments and in the naming of its many public rooms, dining areas, and convention spaces. Circa 1967, $7-9.

Busy Roulette Table, Frontier Hotel and Casino. Circa 1960s, $7-9.

Tall Signage. Frontier Hotel and Casino had one of the world's tallest free-standing signs, costing more than $1 million dollars and rising about two hundred feet in the air in the hotel entrance. It flashed a red carpet welcome to arriving guests, and the huge marquee lists the names of the show business luminaries who appeared in the hotel's showrooms. Circa 1960s, $5-7.

Craps. This lady dice shooter is rooting for a 7 or 11 to appear. Crap tables at Frontier Hotel and Casino were often very busy. Circa 1960s, $7-9.

Memorabilia, Frontier Hotel and Casino. Playing cards ($4-6), $5 gaming chip ($10-15), $1 gaming chip ($3-7), matchbook ($3-12), swizzle stick ($3-6), roulette guide ($1-3), glass ($1-3), pen ($1-3), keno playing booklet ($2-5), keno form ($1-3), and napkin ($1-3). Circa 1960s.

Playing Blackjack, Frontier Hotel and Casino. Circa 1960s, $7-9.

International Hotel and Casino

On July 3, 1969, one day after Landmark Hotel opened, the $60 million International Hotel and Casino opened on Paradise Road, next to the Las Vegas Convention Center. In 1967 Las Vegas financier Kirk Kerkorian bought eighty-two acres of land on Paradise Road for a new project—building the International Hotel, largest hotel in the world. He also bought the Flamingo Hotel, which he used to train employees for his International Hotel.

The massive 1,500-room International Hotel employed 3,000 people and had a large casino. Barbra Streisand was the opening headliner in International's 2,000-seat showroom. Elvis Presley made his great Las Vegas comeback at International during the opening month, and performed there exclusively until his death in 1978.

Dining facilities were abundant at the International Hotel. In addition to the main showroom, there are a number of different gourmet dining rooms each featuring cuisine from a different country—Japanese, Italian, German, or Western. Each was picturesquely decorated in the décor of the country of which its food specialized. The main gourmet room was exquisitely decorated in Egyptian motif.

International Hotel had the world's largest gaming casino. Within the 30,000-square-foot area were 1,000 slot machines, seven poker tables, twelve crap tables, thirty-two blackjack tables, thirteen pan tables, and a one hundred-seat keno lounge.

On the third floor of the hotel was a recreation area containing four tennis courts, a 350,000-gallon swimming pool (one of Nevada's largest), handball and squash courts, shuffleboard and ping pong, a nine-hole putting course, and other activity centers.

International Hotel's enormous showroom was rated among the most luxuriously appointed and certainly the largest in the world. Many stars appeared in this showroom including Peggy Lee, Nancy Sinatra, and the Osmond Brothers. By virtue of its unparalleled capacity it enabled International to book the most expensive star personalities as its main attractions.

By 1971, Kerkorian had sold both the International and Flamingo hotels to Hilton Hotels Corporation. Kerkorian was interested in another venture—building the 2,000-room MGM Grand Hotel.

In 1973, a new 1,674-room wing was added, giving International Hotel (now called the Las Vegas Hilton) 3,174 rooms and making it one of the largest hotels in the world. It remained the largest in Las Vegas for sixteen years until the Flamingo Hilton surpassed it, with 3,530 rooms, and the Excalibur Hotel & Casino, with 4,032 rooms, in 1990.

The Las Vegas Hilton was noted for offering superstar entertainment. It booked some of America's most talked about celebrities, including Bill Cosby, Wayne Newton, Engelbert Humperdinck, Yakov Smirnoff, Crystal Gayle, Ben Vereen, Johnny Cash, Doug Henning, Sandy Duncan, Goldie Hawn, Tony Bennett, Bobby Darin, Perry Como, Donna Summer, Kris Kristofferson, Suzanne Somers, Jim Nabors, Debbie Reynolds, and Tina Turner.

The Las Vegas Hilton has been a leader in helping Las Vegas become recognized as a convention and business travel designation.

International Hotel and Casino. In 1969, Kirk Kerkorian opened the 1,500-room, thirty-stories high, $60-million International Hotel and Casino just off the Las Vegas Strip. The sender of this card wrote, "Are staying here at this hotel. Really having fun!" Cancelled 1969, $10-12.

Largest Hotel and Casino. The world's largest hotel and casino, it was a city-within-a-city. It was also the tallest building in Nevada. Situated next to the Las Vegas Convention Center, International Hotel and Casino was the most magnificent and luxurious hotel-casino in Las Vegas. Circa 1969, $8-10.

Jerry's Nugget Casino

Jerry's Nugget Casino, located at 1821 Las Vegas Boulevard North, started out as the Embassy and Bonanza Clubs. The co-founder of this casino, Jerry Lodge, opened Jerry's Nugget in 1964, after operating a casino in Lovelock, a small town in northern Nevada. Jerry's Nugget has always been a popular North Las Vegas casino with local patrons.

Jerry's Nugget Casino. Opened in North Las Vegas in 1964, the casino was very popular with local patrons. *Author photograph.*

Memorabilia, Jerry's Nugget Casino. Playing cards ($4-6), $5 gaming chip ($8-10), $1 gaming chip ($3-6), 25¢ gaming chip ($20-50), ashtray ($8-10), and keno form ($1-3). Circa 1960s.

Lady Luck Casino

In 1963, Andrew H. Tompkins bought Honest John's Casino, a 2,000-square-foot newsstand and smoke shop with five employees, a few pinball machines, and eighteen slot machines. Four years later, he changed the name of the property, located at Third Street and Ogden Avenue, a block away from the glittering lights of Fremont Street in downtown Las Vegas. Tompkins named his facility the Lady Luck Casino.

In 1972 the Lady Luck Casino added additional table games and offered full gaming. In 1983 the casino became the Lady Luck Hotel and Casino with 112 rooms. In 1985 a sixteen-story, 300-room tower was added along with a renovated gaming floor. A second 25-story tower opened in 1989, which gave the Lady Luck Hotel and Casino a room count of 792, seven hundred slot machines, and 689 employees. In December 1989, the Lucky Dome, a 10,000-square-foot showroom and special events center, opened. "Luck is a Lady," a music, dance, and comedy review show, premiered in the showroom. "Cabaret Circus," produced by Jose Luis Vinas, was the second major show to premiere in the showroom. Melinda "First Lady of Magic" later appeared in the showroom.

The steady growth of this unique gaming establishment can be attributed to several factors. The casino's policy was not only to provide able games and slot machines, but also to involve the players in all kinds of fun and games. There was a tournament of some kind going on at Lady Luck every day.

Honest John's Casino. Located at 304 Ogden Avenue at the corner of Third Street in downtown Las Vegas, Honest John's was a newsstand with slot machines. Andrew H. Tompkins purchased the casino in 1963, changing its name to Lady Luck Casino in 1967. *Author photograph.*

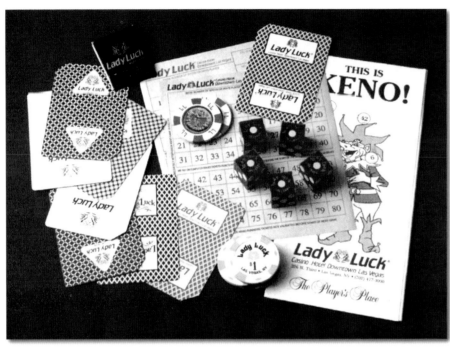

Memorabilia, Lady Luck Hotel and Casino. Playing cards ($4-6), $1 gaming chip ($3-5), set of five matching dice ($5-8), matchbook ($2-4), keno playing guide ($3-5), and keno form ($1-3). Circa 1960s-1970s.

Landmark Hotel and Casino

Landmark Hotel and Casino was a 31-story, 499-room circular tower with its top floors a wide dome suspended in space. It was located at 364 Convention Center Drive, on the corner of Paradise Road and Convention Center Drive, across from International Hotel (now the Las Vegas Hilton) and the Las Vegas Convention Center. It was the tallest structure (356-feet) in Las Vegas, seven feet taller than the downtown Mint Hotel and Casino.

There was a radio commercial about the Landmark. It said, "Say Donald Duck and get a room at the Landmark Hotel for $10." Sure enough, when you said "Donald Duck" at the registration desk, you paid $10 for a room.

In November 1961, developer Frank Caracciolo (also known as Frank Carroll) broke ground for the fourteen-story hotel, modeling it after the Space Needle at the Seattle World Fair. Caracciolo wanted the Landmark Hotel to be the tallest structure in Las Vegas. The Mint Hotel opened in downtown Las Vegas so he added seventeen stories to the original design. In 1966 the tower was still not completed and Caracciolo was short on cash. The Teamsters Union came to the rescue to finish what became a 31-story Landmark; however, Caracciolo was not approved for a gambling license.

Fortunate for Caracciolo and his investors, Howard Hughes was on his Las Vegas property-buying spree. Hughes bought the Landmark Hotel for $17.3 million cash and the former owners were able to pay off their creditors. Landmark was the sixth member of Hughes' Las Vegas empire.

Hughes spent another $3.5 million getting the Landmark ready for its grand opening. Opening day was July 2, 1969. Danny Thomas had the honor of being its opening night star, his second credit of that kind; he had hosted the opening of the Sands Hotel December 15, 1952. Thomas attracted a good opening night crowd in the 31st-floor Top O' the Landmark showroom, with a panoramic view of the city. The Landmark had a 20,600 square foot casino.

Shortly after Landmark's grand opening, it started a slow decline in popularity. Howard Hughes' Summa Corporation finally sold the hotel in 1978. Since then the Landmark changed hands several times and, in 1990, closed its doors and filed for bankruptcy protection. The Las Vegas Convention and Visitors Authority bought the hotel-casino for $15.1 million.

At 5:37 a.m. November 7, 1995, a sad time for many, the Landmark was reduced to rubble by implosion. The implosion was filmed for use in movies.

Today the site is used as a 2,500-car parking lot for visitors to the Las Vegas Convention Center.

Landmark Hotel. The stylized mushroom Landmark Hotel had pie-shaped rooms in its stem and was capped by a lens-shaped capsule with outriggers tapering to fine points. The capsule held the restaurant, bar, and casino. In the 1970s the casino was relocated to the first floor. The Landmark eventually closed in 1991 and was imploded December 7, 1995. Circa 1969, $8-10.

Landmark Hotel and Casino. This 31-story space needle-shaped tower, built by multimillionaire Howard Hughes, had its unveiling in the summer of 1969. It was the sixth family member of the Hughes empire. Danny Thomas had the honor of being its opening-night star. Circa 1969, $10-12.

Memorabilia, Landmark Hotel and Casino. Playing cards ($4-6), $1 gaming chip ($40-120), matchbook ($10-12), keno playing guide ($3-5), keno form ($1-3), and swizzle stick ($3-5). Circa 1969.

Lucky Casino

The Lucky Casino opened in 1963 in the former Lucky Strike Club at 117 East Fremont Street in downtown Las Vegas. In 1967 it became part of the Golden Nugget Gambling Hall, which was located next door.

Lucky Casino. Located at 117 East Fremont Street, the Lucky Casino was a popular casino in downtown Las Vegas. The Lucky Casino, whose high-rise neon façade shot up into a thin tower topping out at 157-feet, had its name sprawled in classy script over orange neon tubing. The colorful sign was designed by Young Electric Sign Company (YESCO) in 1961. In 1967, the Lucky Casino became part of the Golden Nugget Gambling Hall. Circa 1962, $6-8.

Silver Dollar Saloon

The Silver Dollar Saloon, located at 2501 East Charleston Boulevard near downtown Las Vegas, was a small video gaming bar with a scattering of free standing slot machines and a small blackjack pit that usually operated after 4 p.m. daily. Opened in 1964, the Silver Dollar Saloon was in a Las Vegas neighborhood that had one of the city's highest crime rates.

In July 1996 the Silver Dollar Saloon became the Silver Saddle Saloon.

The Silver Dollar Saloon. Located at 2501 East Charleston Boulevard, the Silver Dollar Saloon was a small gaming bar with a few slot machines and blackjack tables. No watered-down country music here. This is a real cowboy bar, with country and western bands playing seven nights a week and a history that dates back to 1931, when it was the Black Cat. *Author photograph.*

Silver Nugget Casino

The Silver Nugget Casino, located at 2140 Las Vegas Boulevard North in North Las Vegas, was opened in 1964 by Major Arteburn Riddle. In April 1966 female blackjack dealers at the Silver Nugget were found to be wearing transparent clothing. The Gaming Control Board saw through it and ordered the owner to "attire all personnel employed in any gaming capacity in decent, modest and proper apparel." The casino went bankrupt and was sold at auction in 1988. In 1990 the casino reopened as Mahoney's Silver Nugget Casino.

Memorabilia, Silver Nugget Casino. Playing cards ($4-6), $5 gaming chip ($8-12), $1 gaming chip ($3-6), 25¢ gaming chip ($2-4), matchbook ($4-12), keno playing guide ($3-5), and keno form ($1-3). Circa 1960s.

Westward Ho Hotel and Casino

In 1961 the casino opened as the Westward Ho Slot Arcade at 2900 Las Vegas Boulevard South north of the Stardust Hotel and Casino and across from the Riviera Hotel and Casino. It became Westward Ho Hotel and Casino in 1971 when table games were added. It was known as the world's largest motor inn.

Cheap drinks, cheap rooms, and cheap food made the Westward Ho popular for many years. The Westward Ho was not considered a fancy casino, but its patrons were always treated very well. The player with $20 in his hand was treated just as well at the Westward Ho as the player holding $1,000 gaming chips in a larger casino. The casino had 949 slot machines, fifteen blackjack tables, craps, roulette, keno, and a wheel of fortune.

The Westward Ho had 777 rooms, a 35,000-square-foot casino, 650 employees, two restaurants, live entertainment in the lounge, a gift shop, and was located on fifteen acres.

The façade of the Westward Ho, remodeled in 1983 by the Young Electric Sign Company (YESCO), was a fantasy design of vinyl umbrella canopies. At night these canopies became dripping fountains of light, their reflective ribbed columns shooting light up from the ground. At the same time light rolls down off the convex surfaces of the umbrellas, appearing ready to drop off on to the pavement in the form of the large bulbs that terminated each umbrella rib.

In 2004 the Westward Ho opened a 13,000-square-foot combination of gas station, convenience store, sports book, restaurant, lounge, and casino at the back of its property along Industrial Road. This mini-casino facility called "The Ho" had a couple hundred slot machines, five blackjack tables, and a sports book. The Ho also had great hotdogs.

Westward Ho closed its doors for good November 17, 2005 to the disappointment of many. It was the end of a "hot dog-and-beer" tradition and another historic piece of Old Vegas trampled away to make room for one more glass-and-steel high rise.

Westward-Ho Slot Arcade. In 1961 a gambling establishment, called the Westward-Ho Slot Arcade, opened at 2900 Las Vegas Boulevard South just north of Stardust Hotel and across from Riviera Hotel on the Strip. In 1971 it became the Westward-Ho Hotel and Casino, with 1,000 rooms and full gaming in the casino. Circa 1970s, $3-5.

Chapter Six:
Fun in the Sun

Engulfed in neon and overwhelmed by sizzling casinos, many visitors to Las Vegas had trouble seeing past the next blackjack table, headline act, or gourmet buffet. Las Vegas was the ultimate circus. But even the most devoted fans of the neon and glitter had to take a break from the gaming action and headliner entertainment.

One glance west by daylight toward Spring Mountains opened up an awe-inspiring world beyond the neon. Where Las Vegas ended, nature began. Dressed in juniper and pine, teeming with burros, home to deer, coyote, mountain lion, and bighorn sheep, bejeweled with Red Rock Canyon's stunning sandstone and Mount Charleston's snow-capped peak, Spring Mountains provided a rich retreat to nature starting just ten miles from Vegas Vic and Fremont Street.

Nearby Hoover Dam was a major sightseeing attraction and Lake Mead was one of several pristinely beautiful recreation areas. Nevada, and neighboring Arizona, offered stunning scenery, whether they ventured just outside Las Vegas or all the way to the Grand Canyon.

The Las Vegas Chamber of Commerce said it best: "Come have fun in the sun!" It was part of an advertising campaign to attract tourists to the desert area for playtime. The weather is perfect almost all year long—sunny days, clean air, and clear skies. Many of the casinos had tennis courts and swimming pools. Horseback riding and golf was also available. Las Vegas was definitely the place to have "Fun in the sun."

Sun Worshippers enjoy Castaways Hotel's Swimming Pool. Circa 1960s, $3-5.

Bedazzling Showgirls Take A Pool Break. Circa 1955, $5-7.

Golf Anyone? When this photograph was taken, the Desert Inn Hotel and Casino was the only resort on the Strip to offer an 18-hole golf course. Wilbur Clark hosted the first nationally televised Tournament of Champions here. Circa 1953, $2-4.

Swimming Pool, Desert Inn Hotel and Casino. Swimming pools were favorite settings for publicity photos. This Olympic size, figure 8 swimming pool at the Desert Inn Hotel and Casino was the center of attraction in its beautifully landscaped patio. Circa 1950s, $4-6.

Swimming Break. Swimming pools would become commonplace in the 1950s motel boom across America, a welcome amenity in Las Vegas' scorching summer heat. No children splashed in this pool at Wilbur Clark's Desert Inn Hotel and Casino; however the three ladies seem to be watching the diving board where the diver is readying for a back flip. Circa 1950s, $6-8.

Beautiful Scenery. The beautiful oasis at the Desert Inn Hotel and Casino, set with lush green lawn on one side and a "Famous Cactus Garden" on the other, invited a relaxing attitude. Circa 1950s, $3-5.

Rooms with a View. Luxurious cabana rooms with sun decks overlooking the spacious Olympic size swimming pool at Dunes Hotel and Casino was a many-splendored setting created for a Goddess where languid loungers lazily confessed "This is Living." Cancelled 1956, $3-5.

An Enjoyable Pasttime. Swimming in the Desert Inn Hotel swimming pool was enjoyed by everyone. This view shows the Skyroom Cocktail Lounge, Painted Desert Room Supper Club, and Lady Luck Bar. Circa 1950s, $4-6.

Colorful Pool Area at the Fabulous Dunes Hotel and Casino. Circa 1960s, $3-5.

Picturesque Beauty. Spectacular beauty was found in the more than 270 acres at Nevada's largest and most deluxe hotel. The figure 8 swimming pool at Wilbur Clark's Desert Inn Hotel and Casino was a year-round attraction. Circa 1950, $4-6.

Garden Area. One of the beautiful attractions at El Rancho Vegas Hotel and Casino was the beautiful garden area pool where year-round swimming was possible because of the temperate desert climate. Circa 1940s, $7-9.

Golf Course. Adjoining the Dunes Hotel and Casino is an 18-hole Championship Dunes "Emerald Green" Golf Course & Country Club. The golf course provided a pleasant respite from the gaming tables. Circa 1960s, $4-6.

First Class Hospitality. El Rancho Vegas Hotel and Casino was famous for first class hospitality and comfort combined with all the excitement of a rip-roaring wide open western gambling town. Circa 1940s, $8-10.

The Fabulous Flamingo Hotel, Looking Across the First Olympic-sized Pool in Nevada. The sender of this card wrote: "Jack Benny and Giselle McKenzie were performing in the showroom." Cancelled 1957, $6-8.

Flamingo Hotel. A view of the grounds of the world famous Flamingo Hotel and Casino, showing the heated Olympic swimming pool in the center of its beautifully landscaped gardens. Cancelled 1951, $6-8.

Swimming and Tennis were Popular Outdoor Activities at Frontier Hotel and Casino. Circa 1960s, $4-6.

Beautiful Sunbathers, Frontier Hotel's Swimming Pool. Circa 1960s, $4-6.

Hacienda Hotel and Casino. Guests could swim in the Olympic size swimming pool or play golf on the night-lighted golf course with a $5,000 Hole-in-One Jackpot. The rooms at this Strip hotel were $10 a day. Cancelled 1960, $6-8.

A Panoramic View. This view shows the glamorous swimming pool at Last Frontier Hotel and Casino. Guests could visit a subterranean room permitting photographs underwater. Circa 1940s, $6-8.

Swimming Pool, Riviera Hotel. Incredibly blue under the brilliant Nevada sun, Riviera Hotel's tremendous pool, surrounded by beautiful French gardens, was delightful year-round. Circa 1950s, $4-6.

Relaxing Poolside. The beautiful Olympic-size Riviera Hotel's swimming pool was where visitors could relax and enjoy the comfort of their own private cabana. Circa 1950s, $4-6.

Summertime Fun. At the Riviera Hotel swimming pool guests could relax poolside or have fun on the diving boards. Circa 1950s, $4-6.

Beautiful Patio and King-size Olympic Swimming Pool. Royal Nevada Hotel became part of Stardust Hotel and Casino in 1959. A diver gets ready for a back flip on the diving board. Copyright 1955, $5-7.

Taking A Dip. Many of these sun worshippers are about to go swimming in the largest temperature-controlled pool in Las Vegas. The Sahara Hotel's main 200,000-gallon swimming pool was bordered by the foliage of the Garden of Allah. Cancelled 1958, $2-3.

Swimming Pool, Sahara Hotel. Set like a royal jewel amid twenty acres of velvet lawn and blossoms, the Sahara's temperature-controlled pool provided endless moments of relaxation and fun beneath the healthful Nevada sun. Circa 1960s, $3-5.

Paradise Pool. The fabulous Sand's Hotel pool, temperature controlled and crystal clear, was where celebrities from the world over were found swimming or lazing around the poolside. Note the diver in mid-air. Cancelled 1965, $4-6.

Glowing Tans. Pale faces were out... glowing tans were in at the Sands' beautiful swimming pool. Lots of activity was going on when this photo was taken. Circa 1950s, $4-6.

Sands Hotel Pool. The sender of this card wrote: "Having a wonderful time. Hot, but so much to see." Cancelled 1963, $4-6.

Craps. A floating crap game in the Sands Hotel swimming pool spread the hotel's slogan, "fun in the sun," around the world. This famous photo was staged in the summer of 1953 by Al Freeman, the public relations director at the Sands. The hotel showed that it would go to any depth to keep its players comfortable by putting a casino annex in the swimming pool. Guests kept cool while playing the hot game of craps. Visored pool mates were the dealers. Circa 1953, $5-7.

Showboat Hotel and Casino. The sender of this card wrote: "Wish the clock didn't go 'round so fast. It's almost time for me to start for home." Check out the poolside service in this view. Cancelled 1963, $5-7.

Enjoying the Nevada Sun at Stardust Hotel's Main Swimming Pool. Circa 1950s, $7-9.

Largest Resort. The world's largest resort, Stardust Hotel and Casino, covered some forty acres of gardens and architectural splendor. This picturesque Big Dipper swimming pool was one of the largest in the west and the adjacent Pool Pavilion offered breakfast, lunch, and light snack service throughout the day. Stardust Hotel had two champion-sized pools. They inherited the second pool when Royal Nevada Hotel became part of the Stardust in 1959. Circa 1960s, $4-6.

Roadside Sign. Behind Stardust Hotel's main swimming pool was the 188-foot-tall Stardust roadside sign. This $500,000 sign, installed in 1965, was a landmark on the Las Vegas Strip. Circa 1966, $3-5.

Swimming Pool and Center Patio, Thunderbird Hotel and Casino. Cancelled 1952, $5-7.

Thunderbird Hotel Showgirls Enjoying their Off-stage Time. Circa 1950s, $3-5.

Swimming Pool, Tropicana Hotel and Casino. Like a sparkling green oasis, the beautiful swimming pool at Tropicana Hotel and Casino drew travelers across the surrounding desert to this fabulous resort in the convention capital of the world. Circa 1960s, $4-6.

Enjoying the Nevada Sun at Tropicana Hotel and Casino. Circa 1960s, $3-6.

Some R&R. An inviting rendezvous for recreation and relaxation at the sparkling half-circle pool at Tropicana Hotel and Casino. Circa 1960s, $3-5.

Chapter Seven:

Entertainment Unlimited

"Only In Las Vegas" is an over-used cliché, but it precisely describes the entertainment that is one of the main reasons millions of tourists come to this resort Mecca every year. No one can dispute Las Vegas' title as "Entertainment Capital of the World," and a look at the marquees on the Strip and downtown shows why. Entertainers are the lure, the magnet, and the essential ingredient of Nevada's gambling industry.

Famous names, superstars, and lavish continental-like productions have been part of the Las Vegas scene since the 1940s. The "Lido de Paris" at the Stardust Hotel, "Folies Bergère" at the Tropicana Hotel, and "Viva les Girls" and "Casino de Paris" at the Dunes Hotel were the standards in Las Vegas for years. The Tropicana's spectacular is still going strong today. These glittering spectacles featured lines of buxom chorus girls, colorful production members and costumes, as well as fascinating specialty acts—magicians, singers, comics, jugglers, and menageries of performing animals.

Press agents or public relations experts are the people who dreamed up words and ideas to promote Las Vegas. During the Golden Years of Vegas these agents introduced many creative, and sometimes wacky, ideas to promote entertainment, gambling, and the hotels in the city.

When Red Skelton made his Las Vegas debut in 1953 headlining the Sahara bill with Anna Maria Alberghetti, the hotel press agent ordered an addition to the Sahara's billboard on the Sunset Strip in Hollywood, a miniature replica of the hotel's Garden of Allah swimming pool. Eight well-chosen young ladies were hired to dive and cavort around the pool eight hours a day in shifts of four hours per mermaid. For some $30,000, the agent caught the fancy of hundreds of potential Sahara Hotel customers.

Other advertising splashes were made using pools in Las Vegas. The Last Frontier built a glass-enclosed observation booth under its pool, fully staffed by cocktail waitresses. In time a slot machine was added underwater as a lead singer from the show dived in with coins and played the machine while photographers snapped cheesecake pictures for nationwide publications.

A classy use of hotel swimming pools occurred at Sands Hotel and Casino during the 1950s. The publicist at the Sands staged a floating crap game. A photograph of this event ricocheted around the world, advertising Sands' slogan "Fun in the Sun" in a captivating manner as guests "got tanned and faded at the same time."

About a year after the Sahara and Sands hotels opened in 1952, there were great rivalries to promote the headliners, much of the blast directed toward the salaries of Marlene Dietrich at the Sahara and Tallulah Bankhead at the Sands. The publicity agent at Sahara pulled one-upmanship on Sands' agent, paying Dietrich $30,000 while Bankhead came off $5,000 less per week. These were enormous paychecks in those years. There was also Dietrich's gown, cunningly designed in beige to appear as if she wore little or nothing above the waist and touted as a "peek-a-boo" costume.

In 1954, movie star Ronald Reagan was entertaining at the Last Frontier. He was paid $5,500 a week, which is $1,650 a week more than he got as President of the United States. But unlike the presidency, Reagan didn't seek his Las Vegas job. He was literally forced into it because of financial woes. Originally he was to play at El Rancho Vegas Hotel, but when he discovered there was a stripper on the program with him, Reagan turned down the El Rancho Vegas offer. Within twenty minutes his agents had a deal at the Last Frontier Hotel. Sharing the program with Reagan were the Continentals, a well-known quartet; the Blackburn Twins, with Evelyn Ward; the Honey Brothers and the Adorabelles; and the house chorus line of Last Frontier. Garwood Van and his orchestra completed the program. *Variety*, the showbiz bible, reviewed the act this way:

> "Ronald Reagan makes his nightly bow here with no particular act, yet the affable film star displays such a winning personality, as he weaves in and out of the show between acts, that his presence gives it a lift into the hit class."

In her first show at the Last Frontier Hotel, Josephine Baker noticed there were no African Americans in the audience. Between shows, she asked what was the hotel's policy regarding African Americans entering the showroom. She was told that they were not allowed. Josephine politely said that if they did not admit African Americans in for the second show, she was going to walk off the stage. When the curtain was raised on the second show, Josephine paused and looked in the audience. In the front row, there was an African American couple sitting at a table. The man was dressed in a tuxedo and the woman was in a lovely evening gown. It was later discovered that the showroom manager pulled a porter and a maid off their shifts and dressed them in formal attire. Later Josephine decided to take a dip in the swimming pool. Immediately after she left the area, the white guests demanded that it be drained. Even though she honored her contract and the pool incident wasn't called to her attention, Josephine Baker never returned to Las Vegas.

Most shows during the 1940s to the 1960s had a dinner performance starting at 8 p.m. The late show was a beverage-only affair and started around 10 or 11 p.m. Several showrooms had a midnight show and some places even had a 2:15 a.m. show.

But all of the entertainment was not in the main showrooms. Most hotels, both on the Strip and downtown, also had lounge-theaters where reservations were not required. Appearing in these spots were many popular entertainers.

Beginning in the 1950s, lounges were used to aid casino traffic, to keep people around the gaming area, and not let them wander too far before hitting another gaming table, wheel, or slot machine. The Last Frontier, in its Gay 90s section, first featured special entertainment, the Mary Kaye Trio. The Sahara Hotel's Casbar was located in an enclosed area at one end the casino. The hottest act during those early years was Louis Prima and Keely Smith. Booked at the Casbar in 1960 was an act that billed itself as Don Rickles and The Franklins. Rickles later graduated from the lounge to the main showroom. Wayne Newton started performing as a lounge act and later earned $150,000 a week in main showrooms.

The Last Frontier Village, adjacent to the Silver Slipper Gambling Hall and next to the Last Frontier Hotel, catered to everyone in the family—from youngsters to grownups. Sure to delight the youngsters was the full-size merry-go-round, scooter ride, or miniature railroad train. In addition there were pony rides during seasonable weather. The Last Frontier Stables was where the stars and entertainers gathered faithfully each week for the "Sunday Morning Breakfast Ride" out past Hoot Gibson's D-4-C Ranch to the mesa or beyond to Red Rock Canyon via horse or stage coach. Years later this western style village became a parking lot for the Frontier Hotel and Casino.

Circus Circus Casino (it would be 1972 before this facility added a hotel) had one of the most unique entertainment policies anywhere, featuring continuous circus acts, aerialists, jugglers, cyclists, clowns, animal acts, and pretty girls offering a three-ring circus on a second-level balcony that overlooked the casino. For grease paint buffs there were also galleries featuring a multitude of midway games. This entertainment is still available at the Circus Circus Hotel and Casino.

All in all there were – and still are – more entertainers and musicians playing before live audiences in Las Vegas than in any other city in the world. A colorful musical cast may feature fifty or more persons on stage, a full orchestra, and many stagehands.

There was something in Las Vegas for everyone when it came to entertainment, no matter the age or personal taste. One visit was hardly enough to scratch the surface. A whole new lineup of famous stars would be in town during a second visit.

Only in Las Vegas is there the variety and round-the-clock tempo of entertainment that keeps pleasing people time after time.

Nat "King" Cole was one of the premier crooners during the 1950s. Everywhere he played he sold out. In 1956, he came to Las Vegas and was offered $4,500 a week to play at the Thunderbird Hotel. Nat could not go into the casino or anywhere else in the hotel except in a sitting area adjoining the kitchen's entrance. After tolerating so many unjust incidents, Nat vowed to never play Las Vegas again unless conditions changed. Two years later, Beldon Katleman, owner of the El Rancho Vegas Hotel, agreed and the next time Nat performed in Las Vegas, he was given the "red carpet" treatment. Frank Sinatra, who liked Nat, also made sure Nat was given full access to the Sands Hotel facilities. The walls of racism in Las Vegas were starting to crumble for everyone.

When the Riviera Hotel and Casino opened on the Strip in 1955 there was a young man performing in the showroom who had worked his way up through the lounges. The entertainment world was shocked to learn that Liberace was paid $50,000 a week for this engagement, tops so far in the accelerating rush of weekly stipends.

Nat "King" Cole was a Nevada entertainer through the 1950s until his death in the mid-1960s. The "schnozzola," Jimmy Durante, was a Nevada star for three decades, beginning after World War II.

After a half-century of performing in all mediums, debonair singer-dancer-actor Maurice Chevalier conducted his first Las Vegas soiree at the Dunes Hotel in 1955. Sophie Tucker, at 71, was appearing at El Rancho Vegas Hotel and marking her 53rd year of entertaining when she helped welcome Chevalier.

The 1960s began with a minimum charge in the showrooms, around $2.50 per person, and rose to an average of $10 at the end of the decade.

The peak of entertainment was achieved in 1963 when Frank Sinatra's Clan descended enmasse upon Dean Martin at the Sands Hotel Copa Room and literally tore the joint apart. Clansmen were Sammy Davis, Jr., Peter Lawford, and Joey Bishop. There were numerous other sudden appearances onstage for about three years and the tales told of the "Rat Pack's" ad-libs are legion. Sammy Davis, Jr., incidentally, was not a total headliner in those years. The billing read "Will Mastin Trio, starring Sammy Davis, Jr." Frank Sinatra and Howard Hughes were not the best of buddies. After Hughes bought Sands Hotel, he cut off Sinatra's credit at the hotel. Frank moved to Caesars Palace, Dean Martin moved to the Riviera, and Sammy Davis, Jr. ended up with his name on the Tropicana Hotel marquee.

Siegfield and Roy arrived in Las Vegas in 1967 to perform as a specialty act in "Folies Bergere" at the Tropicana Hotel. The illusionists, however, were lured back to Paris, France and the "Lido" after just three months in Southern Nevada. They returned to Las Vegas in June 1970 and performed an act in the "Lido" at the Stardust Hotel. They later performed at the MGM Grand Hotel (now Bally's), the Frontier Hotel, and eventually the Mirage Hotel.

The following brief listing during an average three-month period in the 1960s indicates the stature of the entertainers who usually were performing in Strip hotels' main showrooms:

- **Flamingo Hotel** — Dick Shawn, the Cowsills, Juliet Prowse, Don Ho, Tom Jones, Pat Boone, Bobby Goldsboro, and Corbet Monica
- **Frontier Hotel** — Diana Ross and the Supremes, Eddie Fisher, Abbe Lane, Jimmy Durante, Jerry Vale, Phil Harris, and Wayne Newton
- **Riviera Hotel** — Ann-Margaret, Phyllis Diller, Merv Griffin, Connie Francis, and Carol Channing
- **Sahara Hotel** — Jack Benny, Lisa Minnelli, Don Rickles, Bobby Vinton, Buddy Hackett, and Donald O'Conner
- **Sands Hotel** — Vikki Carr, Don Adams, Gloria Loring, Nancy Wilson, Dinah Shore, Nipsey Russell, Alan King, and Dana Valery

A Wild Place. On January 23, the sender of this card showing entertainers in the Ramona Room at Last Frontier Hotel, wrote: "Leaving this wild place for San Francisco, which is probably wilder. Having a good time." Cancelled 1955, $3-5.

New Frontier Hotel and Casino. The resort's world-famous Venus Room featured great entertainers twice a night, seven nights a week. Circa 1958, $3-5.

Showtime. At International Hotel and Casino, a colorful and spectacular time was always had. The main showroom could seat 1,600 people for the dinner show and 2,000 for the late show. Circa 1969, $3-5.

Showtime Redux. At Riviera Hotel and Casino, showtime was always a spectacular occasion and an event long remembered by audience members. Circa 1950s, $2-4.

Showtime. Many Hollywood stars appeared in the Painted Desert Room at the Desert Inn. Show Program cover. Circa 1950s, $10-12.

Copa Room Dinner-Theater, Sands Hotel and Casino. Some of the most exciting stars in the entertainment world appeared in this showroom. Circa 1960s, $2-4.

Broadway Comes to Vegas. Robert E. Griffith and Harold S. Prince, producers of "The Pajama Game," "Damn Yankees," and "Fiorello," presented the Broadway production "Tenderloin," starring Ron Husmann at Dunes Hotel and Casino. Circa 1960s, $5-7.

"Minsky's Girls, Girls, Girls." Appearing in the Fiesta showroom at Fremont Hotel and Casino in downtown Las Vegas, an old-fashioned, new-fangled burlesque, Minsky's combined comedy, music, and a generous helping of beautiful girls. Oversized postcard. Circa 1960s, $6-8.

An All-Star Cast. Hank Henry (birth name was Henry Rosenthal), top banana in the Silver Slipper burlesque shows, appears with second and third bananas and a beautiful gal in a giant champagne glass. The all-star cast of Silver Slipper theater unleashed riotous routines four times nightly without a minimum or cover charge. Circa 1950s, $10-12.

"Nymphs of the Nile." A lavish stage spectacular, starring a Cleopatra's barge-full of perfectly stunning harem maidens and belly dancers, "Nymphs" was presented in the Bagdad Theatre at Aladdin Hotel and Casino. The show was produced by Mitch De Wood and staged and choreographed by Nick Navarro. The cost for the show was $3 per person and included two cocktails. Circa 1960s, $8-10.

The Gaiety Theatre. The burlesque shows in the Gaiety Theatre at the Silver Slipper Gambling Hall were a rich source of music and comedy that kept audiences laughing. The comedy was built around settings and situations familiar to most people. A favorite skit was examining rooms ruled over by quack physicians. Courtrooms, street corners, and inner city schoolrooms were also favorites. Sexual innuendo was always present, but the focus was on making fun of sex and what people were willing to do in pursuit of it. Some examples:

(Injured Man crosses stage in assorted bandages & casts.)

Comic: What happened to you?

Injured Man: I was living the life of Riley.

Comic: And?

Injured Man: Riley came home!

(Minister walks up to a beautiful woman.)

Minister: Do you believe in the hereafter?

Woman: Certainly, I do!

Minister: (Leering) Then you know what I'm here after.

(A buxom Girl drops her purse, Comic tries to return it.)

Comic: I beg your pardon.

Girl: What are you begging for? You're old enough to ask for it.

Many of the burlesque routines spoofed social conventions and linguistic idiosyncrasies. Many involved two men exchanging an intricate series of misunderstood words. A famous example was Bud Abbott and Lou Costello's glorious "Who's On First" baseball skit. A strip tease was often part of a Silver Slipper show, something that vaudeville, film, and radio could not. Circa 1950s, $8-10.

Candy Barr. A stripper, burlesque exotic dancer, actress in one pornographic movie, and model in men's magazines, during the 1950s Candy Barr received nationwide attention for her stripping career. Her trademark costume consisted of cowboy hat, pasties, scant panties, a pair of pearl-handled cap six-shooters in a holster strapped low on her shapely hips, and cowboy boots. She was married in 1959 in Las Vegas while headlining at El Rancho Vegas Hotel and Casino; that same year she was hired by 20th Century Fox Studios as choreographer for "Seven Thieves." She taught actress Joan Collins how to "dance" for her role as a stripper. She returned to Las Vegas in early 1968 and appeared at the Bonanza Hotel and Casino. Candy Barr is among the inductees in the Hall of Fame of Exotic World Burlesque Museum, Helendale, California, halfway between Los Angeles and Las Vegas. Circa 1959, $10-12.

Brochure. Some of the stars that entertained in the Blue Room at the Tropicana Hotel were Louis Armstrong, Count Bassie, Pete Fountain, Al Hirt, Guy Lombardo, Julie London, Boots Randolph, Joe Williams, Roger Williams, Woody Herman, Peter Neor, and Xavier Cugat. Show brochure. Circa 1960s, $8-10.

Lili St. Cyr. El Rancho Vegas Hotel and Casino advertised Lili St. Cyr as the "most beautiful girl in the world." During the 1940s and 1950s, St. Cyr was often called the queen of the striptease. Some remember the suspense of sitting in the audience at the El Rancho Vegas showroom, lights going up, and a dancer performing an act—the likes of which had never been seen before. Those who remember the exotic dances of Lili know that they were just that. While big-busted raunchy girls were swaying hips and twirling tassels in the burlesque houses, Lili St. Cyr was putting in elements of fantasy, mysticism, ballet, and eroticism in her act. Instead of taking it off, Lili was often putting it on — dressing on stage for her audience — and the results were no less tantalizing. On the El Rancho Vegas stage she would perform her staple act of taking a bubble bath on stage and being dressed by a maid for the crowd. She was very popular in Las Vegas. Her act was rivaled by nothing in any burlesque house. Circa 1940s, $10-12.

He was an Actor First. In 1954, film star Ronald Reagan starred in a variety show at Last Frontier Hotel. The future Governor of California and fortieth U.S. President soon gave up acting and performing — and the rest is history. Here he seems to be enjoying the stage with some of Last Frontier's beautifully costumed girls. Circa 1954, $6-8.

Liberace. In 1947, a brilliant young pianist from Milwaukee decided to shed his stage name, Walter Busterkeys, and opt instead for his family name—Liberace. Liberace came to the budding desert gambling oasis and combined flamboyant fashions with mesmerizing music, making him a legend in Las Vegas and around the world. Circa 1960s, $5-7.

Ronald Reagan. Film star Ronald Reagan (center) is seen standing in front of the Last Frontier Hotel's marquee in 1954—long before his political career started. Circa 1954, $6-8.

Entertainment Personified. Few people personify Las Vegas' entertainment heritage more than Liberace. A piano virtuoso trained in the classics, he opted for a career that allowed him to entertain the masses. That decision led him to Las Vegas, where he gained international fame and settled in as one of the city's most popular residents. He was as popular with fellow entertainers as he was with the public. His lavish, outlandish wardrobe became part of his persona. Circa 1960s, $5-7.

Debbie Reynolds. The epitome of her most famous film character, The Unsinkable Molly Brown, Debbie Reynolds was no stranger to the Entertainment Capital. She first performed here with former husband Eddie Fisher at the Tropicana Hotel in 1958 and remained to become one of the city's entertainment legends. For awhile she even owned her own casino (Debbie Reynolds' Hollywood Hotel and Casino) where she performed 20 to 25 weeks a year. She says she has no plans for retirement. "I was always taught there is no word 'can't.' I'd have to be dead to quit." Shown is an autographed Debbie Reynolds postcard of a painting by Ralph Wolfe Cowan. Circa 1993, $20-25.

George Burns and Carol Channing. Appearing in the beautiful Arabian Room at Dunes Hotel, comedian and actor George Burns was best known as a husband and wife comedy duo with Gracie Allen. He made several movies and was well known for his omnipresent cigar, dry wit, and comic timing. Channing was best known for her acting in "Gentlemen Prefer Blondes" and "Hello, Dolly." The sender of this postcard wrote: "Saw this show last night. Everything has been fine so far. We haven't lost much money. Las Vegas has more lights than New York City." Cancelled 1961, $7-9.

Tony Bennett. Starting his singing career in 1949, after twenty years Tony Bennett produced many hit songs, including his most famous song, "I Left My Heart In San Francisco." Bennett is shown with two showgirls in the Arabian Room at Dunes Hotel. Circa 1960s, $7-9.

Eleanor Powell. One of Las Vegas's most exciting moments in 1961 was the return of Eleanor Powell, reputed to be the world's greatest female tap dancer. After a fourteen-year retirement, "Ellie" headlined at Dunes Hotel and Casino in a musical review billed as "An Evening with Eleanor Powell." She was best known for dancing to "Begin the Beguine" with Fred Astaire in the spectacular MGM musical comedy "Broadway Melody of 1940." Circa 1961, $10-12.

Joe E. Lewis. One of the major entertainers at El Rancho Vegas Hotel and Casino throughout the 1940s and 1950s, Lewis' relaxed style embodied the mood of the 1940s night clubbers as they headed out for a night on the town. Lewis was a major influence in popularizing the image of Las Vegas. Circa 1940s, $8-10.

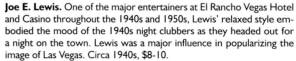

JOE E. LEWIS
Starring at
EL RANCHO VEGAS

The Magnificent
SOPHIE TUCKER

Sophie Tucker. Billed as "The Last of the Red-Hot Mamas," Sophie Tucker's hearty sexual appetite was a frequent subject of her songs, unusual for a female performer of the era. She was the first world-class star to appear in a Las Vegas resort. Her two-week engagement in 1944 at El Rancho Vegas Hotel helped boost the credibility of Las Vegas entertainment. She made many appearances in Las Vegas and enjoyed dishing out some sage philosophy in lyrical style as she sang "Pistol-Packing Mama." Circa 1944, $10-12.

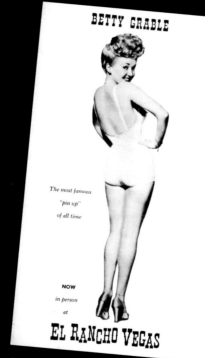

BETTY GRABLE

The most famous "pin up" of all time

NOW in person at

EL RANCHO VEGAS

Betty Grable. In the Opera House at El Rancho Vegas Hotel and Casino in 1956, World War II's Number 1 pinup, Betty Grable, was backed by one of America's leading orchestras, led by husband Harry James and his trumpet. Buddy Rich was on the drums. The James were among the first stars to take up residence in Las Vegas, choosing to live on the Desert Inn Hotel's golf course. Circa 1956, $10-12.

MARILYN MAXWELL
appearing at
EL RANCHO VEGAS

Marilyn Maxwell. A platinum blonde, curvaceous movie actress, and entertainer who appeared in many films and radio programs, Marilyn Maxwell entertained at several Las Vegas hotels. Circa 1950s, $8-10.

LAS VEGAS · NEVADA
EL RANCHO VEGAS

Gloria DeHaven. Singer and film star Gloria DeHaven appeared with one of America's great at

Vic Damone. Singer Vic Damone appeared on the El Rancho Vegas stage where he sang many of his favorite songs. Circa 1950s, $8-10.

VIC DAMONE
now starring at
EL RANCHO VEGAS

Singers and Comics. Singer Julius La Rosa and comedian Buddy Hackett, who was born to be funny, appeared at El Rancho Vegas Hotel with Wanda Smith and her Cover Girls and the Ted Fio Rito's Orchestra. Circa 1950s, $8-10.

WHAT A DOUBLE DATE.....

another wonderful time at

EL RANCHO VEGAS

with

JULIUS LA ROSA

AND

BUDDY HACKETT

ZSA ZSA GABOR

Starring at

EL RANCHO VEGAS

Zsa Zsa Gabor. Though officially an actress, Zsa Zsa Gabor was more famous as a whimsical old-school celebrity sex symbol. Married nine times, Gabor made a career of joking about her man-hungry ways and her love of furs and jewelry. Her film credits include *Moulin Rouge* (1951), *Queen of Outer Space* (1958), and *Touch of Evil* (1959). Zsa Zsa was also the sister of actress Eva Gabor, who played the scatterbrained wife in the 1960s TV ~~Acres~~. Circa 1950s, $8-10.

Eileen Barton. When fabulous singer Eileen Barton went on stage at El Rancho Vegas, she probably sang her 1950 hit song, "If I Knew You Were coming I'd Have Baked A Cake." Circa 1950s, $8-10.

EILEEN BARTON

Appearing at

EL RANCHO VEGAS

Rancho

The Mary Kaye Trio. Mary Kaye, her brother Norman Kaye, and comedian Frank Ross formed the Mary Kaye Trio who were popular in Las Vegas show-rooms and lounges from the 1940s until they broke up in 1966. The trio starred at El Rancho Vegas and was featured at other hotel lounges throughout their career. Circa 1950s, $8-10.

Lisa Kirk. In 1952 Lisa appeared with Ray Bolger as part of the opening night entertainment at the Sahara Hotel and Casino. Circa 1950s, $8-10.

Pat Boone. The second most popular singer of the late 1950s (behind Elvis Presley), Pat Boone sold many records. Comedian/singer Dick Shawn was as off-the-wall as they came and on stage he presented a weird mix of songs, sketches, satire, philosophy, and pantomime. They appeared together at the Flamingo Hotel. Circa 1950s, $8-10.

Pearl Bailey. During Pearl Bailey's performance at the Flamingo Hotel in 1947, she was told she had to find a place to stay in west Las Vegas. She could perform at the Flamingo, but she couldn't sleep there. A little later the Flamingo changed its policy and Pearl, as well as Lena Horne, was able to stay and play there. The following year Pearl performed at El Rancho Vegas. Circa 1947, $10-12.

Switching Places? Two of the nation's orbiting stars checked out each other's style with some role-switching at the Riviera Hotel November 15, 1956. Liberace wore rock' n' roll idol Elvis Presley's zoot suit and strummed his guitar; Elvis responded by putting on the ritz with Liberace's gold lamé dinner jacket while playing the piano. The switch was Liberace's idea, according to *Las Vegas News Bureau* photographer Jerry Abbott, who took the photo. Circa 1956, $5-7.

Donald O'Conner. In 1954 film star Donald O'Conner starred in the showroom at Sahara Hotel and Casino. Circa 1954, $5-7.

Marlene Dietrich. Ringsiders in the main showroom of the Sahara Hotel in June 1959 had an ideal vantage point to check out one of cinema's legends. The glamorous Marlene Dietrich was a favorite star of many Las Vegas visitors. The sender of this postcard wrote: "Here we are having dinner and will soon see my favorite—Marlene. We are having a nice time." Cancelled 1959, $10-12.

Martha Raye. Comedian Martha Raye appeared in the Casbar Theatre at Sahara Hotel and Casino. Appearing in the same program was "Go Go Galore," a sensational Watusi review. Circa 1960s, $8-10.

Teresa Brewer. Beautiful singer Teresa Brewer, along with The Terrytones, appeared at the Sahara Hotel and Casino. Circa 1960s, $8-10.

GOGI GRANT

Mel Tillis and Tammy Wynette. Country singers Mel Tillis and Tammy Wynette appeared at the Frontier Hotel and Casino. Tillis became a hit-making songwriter during the 1950s and won Country Music Association's "Entertainer of the Year Award" in 1976. In 1968, Tammy won the first of three consecutive Country Music Association Female Vocalist of the Year honors. Also in the 1960s, Wynette released the most famous recording of her career, "Stand By Your Man." Circa 1960s, $3-5.

The Rat Pack. Sands Hotel and Casino was home of the famous Rat Pack with Dean Martin, Sammy Davis, Jr., Joey Bishop, Peter Lawford, and the Chairman of the Board, Frank Sinatra. Sinatra and his Clan posed for this photo in front of the Sand's sign and marquee in January 1960 and later performed in the Copa Room. Circa 1960s, $6-8.

Gogi Grant. Singer Gogi Grant, accompanied by a spectacular ice review, performed in the Thunderbird Hotel showroom. In the 1950s Gogi had several hit records: "Suddenly There's A Valley," "The Wayward Wind," "When The Tide Is High," "Who Are We," "You're In Love," and "Strange Are The Ways of Love." Circa 1950s, $5-7.

The Thunderbirds. One of the most spectacular entertainment presentations in the world does not occur in hotel showrooms. It's found in the sky above Las Vegas when the Thunderbird aerial demonstration team is practicing maneuvers. The Thunderbirds, the official U.S. Air Force flying team, are based at Nellis Air Force Base near Las Vegas. The team is often called "the ambassadors in blue" because they represent the U.S. Air Force throughout the world. Circa 1980s, $1-3.

Cyd Charisse. Cast as a French ballerina, Cyd Charisse made her Las Vegas debut in the 1956 MGM musical, "Meet Me In Las Vegas," with Dan Dailey and guest stars Lena Horne, Jerry Colonna, and Frankie Lane. Circa 1956, $5-7.

Entertainment. Entertainers are the lure, magnet, and essential ingredient of the Las Vegas gambling industry. Circa 1960s, $5-7.

Chapter Eight:
Showgirls of Las Vegas

The showgirl has been, for almost seventy years, the most visible symbol of the allure of Las Vegas. She has been the city's most important ambassador to the world, suggesting as she does with her perfect body, long eyelashes, and magnificent costumes that Las Vegas is a dimension beyond the predictable rhythms of everyday life; in other words, the perfect escape.

Throughout the 1950s and into the early 1970s, elaborate French stage productions dominated the Strip. And at the center of the spectacular reviews were icons representing the city's beauty: the Las Vegas showgirl.

Slender and statuesque, these beautiful women who were dressed in rhinestone costumes, feathers, and furs entertained audiences in such shows as "Lido de Paris," "Folies Bergere," "Viva les Girls," "La Parisienne," and "Casino de Paris." The "Lido de Paris" was a hit for more than three decades; "Folies Bergere" is still going strong.

Popular review shows in more recent years were "Beyond Belief" at the Frontier Hotel, "Bal du Moulin Rouge" at the Las Vegas Hilton Hotel, "Hello America" at the Desert Inn Hotel, "Enter the Night" at the Stardust Hotel, "Ziegfeld Follies" at Debbie Reynolds' Hollywood Hotel, "Jubilee" at the MGM Grand and Bally's Grand hotels, "Crazy Girls" at the Riviera Hotel, "Cabaret Circus" at Lady Luck, and "Hallelujah Hollywood" at the MGM Grand Hotel.

"Minsky Goes to Paris" was the first of the "Minsky's Follies" series that debuted January 10, 1957 at the Dunes Hotel. The show was a big hit and enjoyed a four and a half-year run of three presentations a night. The show set a record for attendance in a single week at 16,000. With bumps and grinds in the showroom, gamblers were more than happy to drop money at the crap and roulette tables. "Minsky's Follies" was the first bare bosom stage show in Nevada.

In the 1950s and 1960s showgirls were required to do what was called "mixing" after they performed. This entailed sitting with high rollers and maybe gambling with them. The practice eventually died in the early 1970s, when hotels and casinos stopped catering exclusively to high rollers and began to target dollar bettors.

Showgirls are often the most unappreciated entertainers in Las Vegas. Joan Rivers once said in her nightclub act, "Showgirls are so dumb they can't spell M-G-M," and the audience howled. It's not uncommon for showgirls to be unfairly branded by visiting tourists. Many have found showgirls to be hard-working, professional, amiable, articulate as well as beautiful.

One thing is for certain in Las Vegas: Showgirls have been one of the most enduring images associated with this fabulous city. During the 1950s and 1960s they were the movie stars of the Las Vegas Strip.

Las Vegas Showgirls. They are the American male's eternal fantasy, the symbol of carefree abandon, the centerpiece of glitter, and among the hardest working people in the state. They are Las Vegas' showgirls who come from all parts of the world to break into the entertainment field—from Paris, France to Paris, Kentucky. The world's most beautiful and statuesque girls perform in gorgeously costumed and elaborately staged choreography in the elegant theaters on the Las Vegas Strip and downtown Las Vegas. Circa 1960s, $2-4.

Epitomy of Glamour. The epitome of glamour and sex appeal, the showgirl has long been a fixture in Las Vegas entertainment. Early hotel-casinos such as El Rancho Vegas, Last Frontier, and Thunderbird had chorus lines, but it was the arrival of the Stardust Hotel's spectacular French import "Lido de Paris," in 1958, that gave icon status to the statuesque beauties. Circa 1960s, $5-7.

Showgirls! Las Vegas would not be the same without them. Since the first showgirls began appearing in the 1950s, they have been synonymous with Vegas. They have appeared in scores of famous shows, and in all the famous showrooms in Las Vegas resorts. Circa 1960s, $3-5.

The George Moro Dancers. The 1949 lineup of the George Moro Dancers. Choreographed by George Moro and Ruth Landis, the group was a staple attraction at El Rancho Vegas in the 1940s and 1950s. Circa 1949, $5-7.

Performing at the Flamingo. Backstage it may be pandemonium, onstage it's perfection. That's the drill for some of the most beautiful women in the world, those who earn the title of Las Vegas Showgirl. When house lights dim and the curtain goes up, the city's showgirls lend grace, style, and pizzazz to elaborate production extravaganzas. These showgirls are from a Flamingo Hotel production. Circa 1950s, $5-7.

Dazzling Floorshow. Bright lights, good food, excellent service. The beautiful dancing girls and bright, brief costumes delighted customers in one of the Strip's elegant showrooms. Circa 1960s, $3-5.

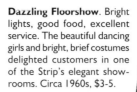

Early Showgirls. What's Las Vegas without showgirls? These were the pre-topless days when flamboyant costumes, a chorus line of well-turned legs, some honky-tonk piano, and a slightly risqué comedian were enough of a show. These dancing showgirls crowd the stage at Last Frontier Hotel for this photo. Circa 1940s, $10-12.

Can Can Dancers. Glorious color and beautiful girls carried on the tradition, started in nineteenth-century Paris, of the popular can-can dance. These can-can dancers are performing at Dunes Hotel and Casino. Circa 1960s, $2-4.

Dance Hall Girls at the Gay 90s Bar, Last Frontier Hotel and Casino. Circa 1945, $5-7.

Colorful Productions. A colorful stage production at the fabulous Flamingo Hotel and Casino where the nation's most popular stage personalities appeared nightly year-round. Circa 1960s, $3-5.

Las Vegas Revues. The Revues followed a typical format, with pretty showgirls wearing elaborate headdresses, feathers around their waists, and little else. Jugglers, magicians, animal acts, or aerialists entertained audiences while sets were changed and showgirls changed into something less. These showgirls are performing at Dunes Hotel and Casino. Circa 1960s, $3-5.

Lavish Shows. The lavish production shows have been a key ingredient in Las Vegas' success for generations, drawing world-class producers, directors, singers, and dancers. The sender of this card wrote: "We had dinner here tonight and saw Ted Lewis and My Shadow. It really was terrific and we enjoyed it very much." Cancelled 1953, $3-5.

Program Cover. Shown is a program cover for the "Revue a la Folies Bergere" show appearing in the Painted Desert Room at Desert Inn Hotel and Casino. This exciting, chic, and entrancing Parisian Revue featured stars of European stages, cafes, and theaters. The production was conceived and staged by Lou Walters, father of television reporter Barbara Walters. Circa 1960s, $10-12.

Lido De Paris

The "Lido de Paris" show, which opened at the Stardust Hotel July 2, 1958 (with Bob Hope and the McGuire Sisters in the audience), performed in the town's largest dinner theater on one of the biggest and most high-tech stages anywhere. A cast of more than one hundred showgirls, dancers, singers, musicians, and specialty acts made up this spectacular show.

The show was created, staged, and directed by Donn Arden, the man who staged and directed the original Lido show in Paris, France. Arden is to stage spectaculars what Cecil B. deMille once was to the film spectacular. He was the first producer to introduce nudity to the American nightclub scene in a manner that was not burlesque. His sharp eye for beauty transcends such experts as Florenz Ziegfeld and Earl Carroll. His topless showgirls are legendary for their beauty, grace, and costuming. His ability to perfectly coordinate the talents of performers and technicians made the "Lido de Paris" a top Las Vegas attraction.

A columnist for the *Las Vegas Review Journal* wrote the following description of a "Lido de Paris" review:

> House light dim, there's a few bars of overture, and from the ceiling of the Continental Cafe descend platforms, each with a bare-bosomed beauty, standing cool as you please, and before the surprise has caused near-sighted gentlemen to repair their thoughtlessness by putting on glasses, the girls are whisked upward into the rafters.
>
> Normally, this would be enough conversation piece to cap any show along the rialto, but the Lido show is full of pleasant surprises. The scenes unfold in sequence, all magnificent in colorful lighting, costumes, and with stirring music... capped by the glories of beautiful girls.
>
> Being bashful by disposition tends to inhibit anything but professional analysis of the plenteous expanse of anatomies presented, but from this layman's corner one can safely say that Pahrump will never be the same.

The "Lido de Paris" show has changed over the years it has been presented at the Stardust Hotel, but it remained essentially the same kind of show featuring gorgeous, nearly nude showgirls, spectacular costumes, equally spectacular scenery, lots of dancers, and sensational stage effects.

Past shows have given the audience the sinking of the Titanic, the explosion of the Hindenburg, the San Francisco earthquake, a thundering flood, and the burning of Moscow by Napoleon—all live and on stage. The Aztec scene that culminated with a great flood of real water thundering over the stage was a very impressive sight and certainly entertaining. Past shows have included many interesting specialty acts including illusionists Siegfried and Roy and their tigers and Bobby Berosini and his Orangutans.

The curtain closed on the "Lido de Paris" show February 28, 1991. It played at the Stardust Hotel for thirty-two years, performing twenty-two thousand shows to around twenty million people. *(Note: The author saw the show fourteen times. Needless to say, it was one of his favorite Las Vegas shows.)*

Stardust. The "Lido de Paris" show debuted on Stardust Hotel's opening day, July 2, 1958, before an audience of seven hundred that included Bob Hope, Harold Lloyd, and the McGuire Sisters. The skaters and hydraulics were impressive, but what really got them talking was something that was missing entirely on many of the showgirls: Brassiers. Stardust Hotel's "Lido" was presented just as it was in Paris and even drew the attention of *Life* magazine in its 1958 Christmas issue. "Lido de Paris" became the show to see. Circa 1958, $2-4.

"Lido de Paris." The French import for Stardust Hotel's opening set the stage for future production shows. The premier edition of "Lido de Paris," the first show ever brought intact from Paris, France to Las Vegas, was titled "Cest Magnifique"—and magnificent it was. Direct from the internationally acclaimed Lido Club on the Champs Elysees, the show boasted a cast of one hundred that did justice to the town's largest showroom, the 700-seat Café Continental theater-restaurant. The Lido appealed to all show goers, regardless of background or homeland; it was 1 hour and 45 minutes of nonstop excitement that included a dazzling array of lighting effects, costumes, music, color, and choreography. Circa 1959, $2-4.

Las Vegas versus Broadway. In the late-1950s and 1960s, a spectacular Las Vegas show cost more than a Broadway musical. The casinos didn't actually make money on the shows, but show goers had to walk through the casino to get to the showroom and back through the casino on the way out. The idea was to draw customers to the gaming tables. This scene is from the "Lido de Paris" at Stardust Hotel and Casino. Cancelled 1967, $2-4.

Grabbing the Audience's Attention. Scantily-clad girls dance for the audience's attention in Stardust's "Lido de Paris" show. Everybody paid attention. The showgirls in the "Lido de Paris" review wore glamour costumes made in Paris, France. They included many feathers and real fur—a lot of fox. You couldn't do that today. The beaded costumes were often very heavy and frequently included large, ornate headpieces that were heavy and difficult to balance. Circa 1960s, $2-4.

The Sixth Edition. A Show Program Cover of the sixth edition of the "Lido de Paris" review, conceived by Pierre Louis-Guerin and Rene Fraday, and staged and directed by Donn Arden. Circa 1966, $10-12.

Popular Show. Some 20 million guests have seen the spectacular "Lido de Paris" show at Stardust Hotel and Casino. Feathers, long eyelashes, and sparkle are all part of the Las Vegas showgirls' every-night makeup. Circa 1960s, $2-4.

Show Program Cover. Circa 1960s, $10-12. A *Las Vegas Sun* columnist wrote of his initial reaction to "Lido de Paris:"

"Now the stage came alive. A lot of naked chests, attached to pretty gals, came down on elevators from the ceiling. Other naked chests, attached to other pretty girls, made up the backdrop. They came up from sunken stages and off the wings. In a couple of minutes a curtain went up revealing a huge swimming pool and some more naked mermaids."

"Lido" at Stardust. Each evening, as the curtain went up in the Café Continental, another audience was thrilled by the spectacular "Lido de Paris." Breaking every attendance record in the entertainment capital of the world, the Stardust Hotel extravaganza went through many editions. The stage of the Café Continental was ideally suited for the world-famous Lido. Swimming pool, ice rink, dazzling sets that changed with each magnificent production... all were used to create unparalleled effects for one of the most magnificent floorshow ever presented. Show Program Cover. Circa 1960s, $8-10.

Folies Bergere

Las Vegas visitors have been watching the "Folies Bergere" show at the Tropicana Hotel since it opened in 1959. From its beginning, "Folies Bergere" boasted a variety of beautiful showgirls in dancing and singing roles. There were also the specialty acts—jugglers, magicians, acrobats, mimes, and clowns. On the roster of shows that have played Las Vegas since the era of the fun-filled fifties, none have been continuously running longer than "Folies," which was brought to the Tropicana from Paris, France. Its enduring appeal has spawned a host of imitators that eventually wore out or were sent packing for a variety of reasons even as "Folies Bergere" continues churning forward. The show is an entertainment icon.

The "Folies Bergere" show was based on a similar 1869 show that appeared in Paris. The dazzling display of color and motion that painted the "Folies" stage nightly – the beautiful showgirls, dancers, and costumes – became the toast of Paris. The "Folies" became the center of world attention as an entertainment spot for fostering new and upcoming stars. It attracted variety acts and talented young artists from around the world, people such as Josephine Baker, Maurice Chevalier, the Marx Brothers, and Charlie Chaplin. All made their claim to fame under the marquee of the "Folies." The first nude showgirl appeared on the "Folies" stage in the early 1900s. The naughty "Folies Bergere" became famous for its bare beauties at the turn of the century. By 1918, the nude showgirl had become the main box office attraction. Today in Las Vegas, the showgirls are still a featured party of the "Folies Bergere" as it is presented at the Tropicana Hotel.

Illusionists Siegfried and Roy got their start in Las Vegas as a specialty act in the "Folies Bergere." The notion that magic could be used as the basis for a major show was treated as something of an illusion in those days. Magic was not supposed to be something show goers cared about. But the "magic" of the "Folies" has been producing satisfying results for years. It really works. Siegfried and Roy went on to perform at the Stardust, MGM Grand, Frontier, and Mirage hotels.

A mishap occurred in one of the "Folies" that Siegfried and Roy appeared in. They were going through one of their illusions involving large wild animals. A panther suddenly got loose and jumped into the open orchestra pit. All of a sudden there was this panther in the small area right under the stage with the orchestra. Of course, the animal was as scared as anyone else and fortunately no one nor the animal was hurt, but probably some of the musicians produced a few sour notes.

Another magic act appeared at the Tropicana Hotel. For ten years Lance Burton was a featured specialty act in the "Folies" and was one of the better arguments for visitors seeing the show. Burton went on to star in his own magic shows at the Hacienda Hotel and later the Monte Carlo Hotel, where he is still performing.

The Sensational Cavarettas were another popular specialty "Folies" act. For several years, the Cavarettas, a daring aerial adagio, performed on a single stationary trapeze. They combined grace and sensuality with high act feats that were executed twenty-eight feet above the stage floor. For eight minutes of every "Folies Bergere" performance, the Cavarettas left the audience breathless.

"Folies" showgirls parade across the stage wearing headpieces and costumes that weigh as much as thirty pounds a piece and cost as much as $5,000.

One of the most popular parts of a "Folies" show is the "Can-Can" finale. It features ten minutes of exciting dancing and acrobatics. Over the years it has won several awards as the best production number in any revue on the Strip.

Even though there are many different acts in every show, the "Folies Bergere" is still most famous for its tall, statuesque showgirls, its storybook theme, and Music Hall format.

Lavish Production Shows. The Las Vegas lavish production shows set the standard for the entertainment industry. The extravaganza, "Folies Bergere," featured more than fifty beautiful showgirls wearing hundreds of rhinestone-studded costumes. This dazzling show produced the type of entertainment that tourists wanted to see when they came to the Entertainment Capital of the World. Circa 1960s, $2-4.

"Folies Bergere." Long before Americans set eyes on the "les femmes" of "Folies Bergere" during the 1950s, the famed French revue had already replaced Moulin Rouge as the spicy haunt favored by European royalty and aristocracy who made Paris their playground. Since its opening in 1869, the extravaganza has been performed more than 35,000 times for more than 50 million people on its Paris stage and at its American home, Tropicana Hotel and Casino. It's regarded now as much a French national institution as the Eiffel Tower or the Louvre. Show Program Cover. Circa 1950s, $8-10.

A Colorful History. Showgirls have a long and colorful history in Las Vegas. They are perhaps the most envied, and most misunderstood, of the city's entertainment scene. The job is much more rigorous than many would imagine. If you doubt it, try spending ninety minutes on stage, twice a night, in high heels, wearing a headdress or sequined costume that might weigh as much as seventy pounds. Shown here, among the most famous, were showgirls from the "Folies Bergere" show at Tropicana Hotel. Circa 1960s, $2-4.

"Show of Shows." So successful has been this "show of shows" that such offerings as the Ziegfeld Folies, the Rockettes, "Lido de Paris," and "Casino de Paris" all can trace their ancestral beginnings to "Folies Bergere." Show Program Cover. Circa 1950s, $8-10.

"Folies Bergere." Internationally celebrated as a rendezvous for recreation and relaxation, Tropicana Hotel and Casino was famed for the splendor of "Folies Bergere." The lovely mannequins and dancers of "Folies Bergere" are shown with Maurice Chevalier in a scene from the George Sidney International-Posa Films International Production "Pepe," filmed at the Tropicana Hotel. "Pepe," a Columbian release in CinemaScope and color, starred Cantinflas, Dan Dailey, and Shirley Jones and presented many guest stars as well as the "Folies Bergere" beautiful showgirls. Circa 1960s, $3-5.

Program Cover. This version of the "Folies Bergere" at Tropicana Hotel and Casino starred Audrey Arno who had come direct from a record-shattering engagement in the renowned Eiffel Tower in Paris, France. Making her American debut, the vibrant singer-dancer was the first performer ever to receive "star" billing since "Folies Bergere" was brought to Las Vegas. Show Program Cover. Circa 1960, $10-12.

A Star is Born. While the "Folies" at the Tropicana Hotel is noted most for its compatible offering of enticing females, spectacular staging, and exciting specialty acts, it has also fostered its share of stars... Charlie Chaplin, Maurice Chevalier, Fernandel, Patachou, Pavlova, Mistinguett, and Josephine Baker. Show Program Covers. Circa 1960s, $8-10.

Casino De Paris

The 700-seat main showroom at the Dunes Hotel, called the Casino de Paris, housed the French spectacular of the same name that was presented twice nightly—7:45 and 11:45. The show was imported from Paris, France with a cast of one hundred continental artists and featured some of the most beautiful showgirls in the world. The spectacular review was conceived, produced, and directed by Frederic Apcar. The "Casino de Paris," opening December 17, 1963, was the Dunes' answer to the trendy, European-style reviews popularized by the Stardust Hotel and its 1958 "Lido de Paris" show and the Tropicana Hotel and its 1959 "Folies Bergere."

"Casino de Paris." Opening December 17, 1963, "Casino de Paris" was Dunes Hotel and Casino's answer to the trendy, European-style revues popularized by Stardust Hotel and its 1958 "Lido de Paris" show. Circa 1963, $10-12.

Spectacular Show. The "Casino de Paris" spectacular at Dunes Hotel and Casino had a cast of one hundred continental artists and featured some of the most beautiful girls in the world. The show was presented twice nightly, 7:45 and 11:45 p.m. Circa 1960s, $13-15.

See Show, Then Gamble. The performances of the "Casino de Paris" showgirls brought gamblers into Dunes Casino. Many of them would stay and play craps and roulette after the show. Circa 1960s, $8-10.

Showgirls from "Casino de Paris," Dunes Hotel and Casino. Circa 1960s, $5-7.

Chapter Nine:
Las Vegas After Dark

Las Vegas and Neon became synonymous in the 1950s and 1960s. "Glitter Gulch," or downtown, became so bright that you could hardly tell night from day. The black desert sky, along the Las Vegas Strip became the undisputed brightest stretch of road in the world. Maybe neon could be neon without Las Vegas, but Las Vegas could never be Las Vegas without neon.

Neon invaded Las Vegas with a vengeance. Its artistry benefited enormously by the local tradition of one-upmanship, inspired by the fierce competition between the major hotels and casinos.

The Young Electric Sign Company (YESCO), originally a Salt Lake City company, started building Las Vegas' neon marvels in the 1930s. The town's first neon sign was a freestanding, forty-foot sign with vertical letters, topping a bright marquee, for the Boulder Club. YESCO opened a facility in Las Vegas and became the city's oldest sign-making company. The designers at YESCO can be credited with elevating neon signage to an art form. They have produced almost seventy-five percent of the town's neon favorites and best-loved images; Frontier Club, Sal Sagev Hotel, Pioneer Club, Caesars Palace, Las Vegas Club, Eldorado Club, El Cortez, El Rancho Vegas, Golden Nugget Gambling Hall, and many more. The Golden Nugget sign took the early prize with a blindingly bright sign that remained downtown's centerpiece for nearly fifty years. In 1951 YESCO built "Vegas Vic," Nevada's 75-foot, 12,000-pound cowboy that was installed over the Pioneer Club in downtown Vegas. This massive sign had articulated arms and a voice that welcomed tourists with "Howdy Podna!" Also in 1951, YESCO designed the sign for the Horseshoe Club. In 1956 the Fremont Hotel and Casino sign went up and, a year later, Mint Casino started shining over Fremont Street. The company used a shoe of the company's payroll clerk as the model for the revolving Silver Slipper Gambling Hall sign.

In 1958 YESCO erected the largest sign, for that time, in Las Vegas on the Stardust Hotel. This massive sign fascia covered the entire front of the building. It boasted thousands of flashing lights bulbs and neon tubes, simulating stars and planets against a painted lunar background. This 200-foot long and thirty-foot high sign had a gleaming earth turning in a welter of planets, comets, and flaring meteors.

In 1966 the Frontier Hotel and Casino installed the tallest sign in the world, 184 feet. Then the Sahara Hotel and Casino built a sign thirty-six feet taller. And the signs kept getting bigger and bigger and taller and taller.

Many of the early casinos have come and gone, or signs were replaced with newer neon. Many of the older signs are now resting in the YESCO graveyard, where the neon of Las Vegas comes to die: the old Sahara Hotel sign, the Golden Nugget, the Dunes. This graveyard can really take you back in time. Other old neon signs may be found in the Neon Museum on Fremont Street in downtown Las Vegas. The Hacienda Horse and Rider sign is the centerpiece of the museum.

Nighttime in Las Vegas was party time. As the lights flashed over the hotels and casinos, many visitors headed for the hotel lounges for a drink and to rehash the day's activities with old or newfound friends and to watch the lounge entertainment or to catch one of the spectacular shows in the hotel's showroom. Other visitors headed for the casinos to take their chances with "lady luck."

The Lights Standout. A gleaming jewel in the desert, the neon-lighted casinos and entertainment spots of Las Vegas beckon to all in search of fun. Circa 1940s, $14-16.

Hotel and Casino Marquees: A Work of Art. Circa 1951, $10-12.

Looking West on Fremont Street, Downtown Las Vegas. This was known as the Casino Center. Shown on the left, the Golden Nugget Gambling Hall, Lucky Casino, and Pioneer Club; on the right, Binion's Horseshoe Hotel and Casino, Mint Casino, and the Las Vegas Club. The sign for the Union Plaza Railroad Depot is shown at the end of Fremont Street. Circa 1960s, $3-5.

Looking East on Fremont Street, Downtown Las Vegas. This famous resort area has skyscraper hotels, world renowned restaurants, headline entertainment, and all forms of gambling twenty-four hours a day. Circa 1960s, $3-5.

The Boulder Club. Located in downtown Las Vegas, the Boulder Club advertised roulette, slot machines, 10¢ craps, and 21. This forty-foot sign was installed by Young Electric Sign Company (YESCO). The Boulder Club was the oldest club in Las Vegas. It never closed. Circa 1947, $8-10.

Beautiful Setting. One of the many beautiful desert sunsets that fall over the glittering city of Las Vegas. In the distance are hotel-casinos along the Las Vegas Strip. Circa 1960s, $1-3.

Entrance, Caesars Palace Hotel and Casino. The colorful entrance of Caesars Palace Hotel and Casino as seen at night from the Las Vegas Strip. The spectacular fountains and illuminated Italian statuary made this a sight long to be remembered. Caesars Palace was a swinging palace of pleasure, rendezvous for lively people, and tops for real action. Star-studded floor shows, luscious gourmet food and glittering nightlife. Circa 1960s, $3-5.

Nighttime View, Circus Circus Casino. The "Big Top" death defying trapeze acts and continuous entertainment that occurred in this casino were enjoyed by people of all ages. Circa 1969, $6-8.

Lighting Up the Strip. This beautiful roadside sign helped light up the Las Vegas Strip at night. Installed in 1966, the sign contained 10,000 lighting units and cost Dunes Hotel and Casino $47,500 a year to operate. Circa 1960s, $3-5.

Nighttime View, Hacienda Hotel and Casino. This view shows its palomino and caballero neon sign. Today this beautiful sign can be seen in the Neon Sign Museum in downtown Las Vegas. Circa 1960s, $5-7.

Fremont Hotel and Casino. Centered in the glittering excitement of downtown Las Vegas, Fremont Hotel and Casino offered fine accommodations, superb dining, and dazzling entertainment. When this photo was taken the hotel's marquee was advertising the "Minsky's Girls, Girls, Girls" show in the theatre-restaurant. Circa 1950s, $3-5.

Bright Spot. This is the "bright spot" on the world's brightest two blocks, featuring seven miles of neon and 28,000 bulbs at Binion's Horseshoe Hotel and Casino. When this photo of the Horseshoe was taken, it had one hundred guest rooms, three cocktail bars, 24-hour restaurant, and a 'round-the-clock casino. Circa 1960s, $3-5.

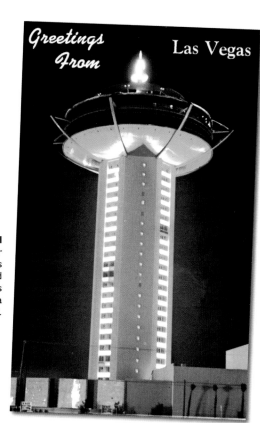

Night View, Landmark Hotel Tower. Patrons had a spectacular view of the bright lights of the Las Vegas Strip. Its lavish casino and restaurants provided visitors lots of fun and entertainment. Circa 1969, $3-5.

The Las Vegas Club Hotel and Casino. Occupying the former site of the Overland Hotel at the corner of Main and Fremont streets, the neon at this facility helped light up the western end of Fremont Street. Circa 1960s, $3-5.

Night View, Mint Hotel and Casino. Circa 1960s, $3-5.

The Nevada Club. Located at 113 East Fremont Street, it was between the Lucky Strike and California Clubs. Circa 1956, $3-5.

Largest Mechanical, Neon-Lighted Sign in the World. The Howdy Podna of Las Vegas greeted visitors to the famous Pioneer Club. Vegas Vic was a landmark sign in downtown Las Vegas. Circa 1951, $5-7.

Riviera Hotel and Casino. Looking at the Riviera Hotel and Casino from behind the fountains at Circus Circus Casino. Circa 1960s, $1-3.

All Night Long. The Sands Hotel's roadside signboard got the attention of anyone passing on the Las Vegas Strip all night. Circa 1960s, $3-5.

Royal Nevada and Casino. Opened in 1955, Royal Nevada was a popular hotel of beautiful design. In 1959 this hotel-casino became part of Stardust Hotel and Casino. Circa 1955, $4-6.

Sands Hotel and Casino. One of the most beautiful and ultra modern resorts on the Las Vegas Strip, its modern styled architecture and height changed the Las Vegas skyline. The gleaming tower at Sands Hotel became a showplace during the evening hours. Circa 1960s, $5-7.

Hotel Showboat, Las Vegas, Nevada

Nighttime View. At night the Showboat Hotel and Casino looked like a Steamboat sailing the Mississippi River. Circa 1950s, $6-8.

The Silver Slipper. In 1950 it would be hard to miss the huge turning slipper sign at the Silver Slipper Gambling Hall. Circa 1950, $5-7.

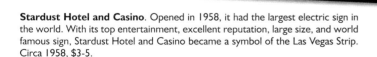

Stardust Hotel and Casino. Opened in 1958, it had the largest electric sign in the world. With its top entertainment, excellent reputation, large size, and world famous sign, Stardust Hotel and Casino became a symbol of the Las Vegas Strip. Circa 1958, $3-5.

New Signage. In 1965 Stardust Hotel and Casino added a new 188-foot-tall free-standing roadside sign. It cost $500,000 and at night the effect was mesmerizing. Its constellation of neon and incandescent bulbs made it appear that lights were sprinkling from the stars, showering down upon the sign. It became the most stunning sign along the Strip. Circa 1965, $5-7.

Chapter Ten:
Gambling

Entertainment, excitement, sun and fun: these are just a few of the reasons why millions of visitors come to Las Vegas each year. Still, with all Las Vegas has to offer, casino games have always been the city's number one attraction.

Some games that were found in the early casinos should be dismissed as "bait," games that no informed gambler would dream of playing. Don't blame the casino owner for having them. A good part of the wear-and-tear on the casino's thick carpeting comes from the shoes of "lookers," tourists who are out to see the sights and get anything for nothing that's available.

There are a lot of them in Las Vegas casinos, watching the shows, eating the 69¢ breakfast, maneuvering an occasional free drink, crowding around the players for further free entertainment, and having themselves a great time without any expenditure.

When they decide to gamble a couple of dollars, to have something to talk about when they go home, they almost invariably gravitate to the Wheel of Fortune, chuck-a-luck, or some other come-on. However, the favorite come-on of all times has been slot machines.

When legalized gambling got underway in Las Vegas in 1931 the favorite games of chance attracting players were the usual card games: blackjack, baccarat, poker, pan, faro, and three-card monte. There were also bingo, keno, chuck-a-luck, roulette, craps, the wheel of fortune, and, of course, slot machines. Chuck-a-luck, commonly called the birdcage, and the wheel of fortune, also called the big six wheel, were often found near the entrance of the casino to lure players who were attracted to these games. Faro, pan, and Monte ceased to exist after a few years. They were regarded by the operators as low-earning games where the house could not even afford to pay the dealer. By the mid-1950s there were only a half dozen faro games in Las Vegas casinos.

This chapter contains a brief description of some of the casino games that were played through the 1930s to the 1960s.

Superstar Entertainment. Year-round outdoor recreation. Boxing matches. Sporting events. Las Vegas is known around the world for many things, but none are more famous, or more responsible for its constant pulse of excitement, than the thrilling casino games that are the heart of the Las Vegas experience. Casino games are the number one attraction for the millions who visit this exciting city each year. Cancelled 1963, $2-4.

Games of Chance. The popular casino games played in Las Vegas during the 1930s-1960s were baccarat, bingo, blackjack, craps, faro, keno, roulette, slot machines, and wheel of fortune. Circa 1960s, $7-9.

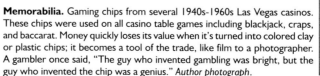

Memorabilia. Gaming chips from several 1940s-1960s Las Vegas casinos. These chips were used on all casino table games including blackjack, craps, and baccarat. Money quickly loses its value when it's turned into colored clay or plastic chips; it becomes a tool of the trade, like film to a photographer. A gambler once said, "The guy who invented gambling was bright, but the guy who invented the chip was a genius." *Author photograph.*

Baccarat

The ancient game of baccarat is an easy game to play since there are only two propositions to bet. The object of the game is to bet on the hand whose total count comes closest to the number "9." A gambler may bet on either the Banker's or the Player's hand at any time before the cards are dealt. Baccarat is played with eight decks of standard playing cards. The cards are shuffled by the croupier or dealer and then placed in a box called the "shoe." The croupier controls the entire game. Two hands are dealt from the shoe, one for the Banker's Hand and the other for the Player's Hand. The count and number of cards dealt to each hand are governed strictly by a simple set of rules. Tens and picture cards and any combination of cards totaling ten count nothing. An Ace is counted as one. The two through nine cards are counted at face value.

Bingo

Bingo was played in several early Las Vegas casinos. Players bought cards with numbers on them corresponding to the five letters in the word B-I-N-G-O. Numbers such as B-2 or N-34 are then drawn at random until one player completes a "BINGO" by covering five numbers in a vertical, horizontal, or diagonal row on one of their cards. Variations and payouts varied from Bingo Parlor to Bingo Parlor.

Dunes Hotel and Casino. Baccarat players wagering in the splendor of Dunes Hotel and Casino. The highest of high rollers often played in separate casinos, or private parlors, isolated from the hubbub of the main casino floor. In baccarat, players bet on one of the following outcomes: the player will win; the bank will win; or there will be a tie. Note that the players are using paper bills instead of gaming chips. Circa 1960s, $7-9.

Blackjack

Blackjack, also known as 21, has always been one of the most popular games in a casino. The dealer starts the game by dealing each player two cards. In some casinos, they are dealt to the player face up, in others face down, but the dealer always gets one card up and one card down. Everyone plays against the dealer. The object is to get a total that is higher than that of the dealer without exceeding 21. All face cards count as 10; all other number cards, except Aces, are counted at their face value. An Ace may be counted as 1 or 11, whichever the player chooses it to be.

Starting from the dealer's left, additional cards are given to the players who wish to draw (be "hit") or none to a player who wishes to "stand" or "hold." If the player's count is closer to 21 than the dealer's, then the player wins. If the count is less than the dealer's, the player loses. Ties are a push and nobody wins. After all the players are satisfied with their counts, the dealer's facedown card is exposed. If the dealer's two cards total 16 or less, the dealer must "hit" (draw an additional card) until reaching 17 or over. If the dealer's total exceeds 21, then all players whose hands have not gone "bust" are paid.

Blackjack. An exciting game that's easy to understand and fun to play is Blackjack; it's sometimes profitable, sometimes frustrating, but a game where players can keep track of the cards and use their skill to attempt to win. Shown, players at Circus Circus Casino. Circa 1968, $4-6.

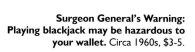

Surgeon General's Warning: Playing blackjack may be hazardous to your wallet. Circa 1960s, $3-5.

Chuck-A-Luck

Chuck-a-luck was played with three large dice tumbled in a bottle-shaped wire cage called "chuck cage." The players placed their bets on a layout, a table with spaces marked from 1 to 6. If the player's number appeared on one die, the casino paid off even money; if his number appeared on two dice, the casino paid 2 to 1; and if on all three dice, 3 to 1. Several of the Las Vegas casinos had different table layout designs. The game was of minor importance because it was seldom played for high stakes. In 1954 there were less than a dozen chuck-a-luck games in Las Vegas casinos.

Craps

Craps has always been a popular game in Las Vegas casinos. It is a fast action game that offers players a wide variety of bets with different payoff odds when a player wins. Craps is played with two dice on a large table that has a colorful layout to indicate the various permissible wagers.

The rules for craps originated centuries ago in France. On the first toss, the player wins on a 7 or 11 (a natural) and loses on a 2, 3, or 12 (craps). When any other number comes up, the player can still win by rolling this "point" again before throwing a 7, which changes from a natural on the first (or come out) roll to a loser on all others.

Casino players can bet on either a win by putting chips on the Pass Line, or a loss, on the Don't Pass Line. Once the shooter has a point to make, any player can also bet Come or Don't Come. On those bets the next toss of the dice is treated as the start of a new roll. So the Crap table may in effect have half a dozen dice games going on at once.

When a player bets the Pass Line, the house has a 1.4% edge because shooters lose slightly more often than they win. The house edge can be reduced to less than 1% if the player takes Odds on the Pass Line bet. After a point is determined, a player can make an additional bet in support of the original Pass Line bet. The same rule for taking or laying the Odds applies to Don't Pass, Come and Don't Come bets.

Crap tables also offer a complex array of side bets—wagers that certain numbers or combinations will show up on later tosses.

Faro

Las Vegas casino owners breathed a collective sigh of relief when faro gasped its last breath as a casino game—not because they had lost great sums of money to faro players but because the game simply did not pay

its way. In the 1950s and mid-1960s, faro was still being played at the Horseshoe Club, the Las Vegas Club, The Dunes Hotel, the Aladdin Hotel, and the Stardust Hotel. In the time since then faro has completely vanished from our midst.

Faro was played on a table with a few accessory items by any number of players, and with three representatives of the casino to manage the game. The game employed a layout of thirteen cards, from Ace down to Deuce. Players put their bets on individual cards. A shuffled deck was put into a shoe and the dealer dealt one card at a time from it. The first card meant nothing, but after it, the second card was a loser and the third card was a winner, until only three cards are left. If the dealer turned two consecutive cards of matching value, he got half of whatever was bet on that card.

Faro was the champion time-killer of casino gambling. It was sometimes called "Buckin' The Tiger."

Keno

The game of keno originated in China 2,000 years ago. It was an uncomplicated way to relax and gamble. On a blank keno ticket the player marked from 1 to 20 numbers (out of 80) with a crayon. The player gave the marked ticket and bet to an agent at the keno counter or a keno runner. Within a few minutes, the casino would select at random 20 of the 80 numbers. The player compared these numbers to the numbers he selected. The amount of money a player would win depended on how many of his numbers were selected and the type of ticket he played. If he picked 8 numbers out of 8, he won $25,000. Unfortunately, his odds of doing that were 230,000 to 1. There are many different ways to bet a keno ticket.

Poker

Poker conjures up images of saloons in the old West where hustlers and gun fighters did battle. When gambling was legalized in Las Vegas in 1931, playing poker was not so risky. Players could lose their stakes, but at least they stayed alive. Variations on the game, with their own rules, were adapted for casinos. Types of poker played in casinos include Five-card draw, Seven-card stud, Texas hold 'em and Omaha. High-stakes poker games require nerves of steel, a cool head, and an inscrutable countenance if a player is to outwit his equally cunning opponents.

Craps. The 1949 *Golden Nugget Gaming Guide* describes craps as the game for red-blooded HE-men and SHE-women! It's fast, furious, and fun. Easy to play when you only play the best bets. It's the most popular action game in the casino. The craps game shown is taking place at Circus Circus Casino. Circa 1968, $4-6.

The Poetry of Probability. Part of the appeal of casinos is the infinite possibilities and the wonder of the numbers. The games have captivated people throughout history. Roulette may be the prettiest and most colorful game of chance in any casino. It's not a game that requires great skill; it's a game of luck. Despite the leisurely pace, it can be a thrilling game. Here gamblers play roulette at the Circus Circus Casino. Circa 1968, $1-3.

The Best Tables. Are some crap tables better than others? Yes! And they're always the ones you're not at and can't get to because they're too crowded. But when you do get there, the crap table you left instantly becomes better. Circa 1960s, $3-5.

Roulette

Roulette is a fascinating game that provides exciting action with its spinning wheel and bouncing white ball. It also offers players many different types of bets and payoffs.

Roulette is a colorful and exciting game to watch. The wheel spins and a ball bounces around, finally dropping into one of the slots, numbered 1 to 36, plus 0 and 00, at odds of 35 to 1. Or they can bet on two adjoining numbers (17 to 1), or groups of three, four, five, six or twelve numbers (at odds ranging from 2 to 1, to 11 to 1). Or they can bet even money that the ball will stop on the Red or Black, the Odd or Even, the Low 18 numbers or the higher ones.

Slot Machines

In 1899, Charles Fey of San Francisco devised the Liberty Bell, the forerunner of modern slot machines. The coin-operated slot machine had a basic design of three spinning wheels marked with symbols. In 1905, the Mills Novelty Company of Chicago stole a machine and copied the design and, soon afterward, other companies began producing similar products. Slot machines spread rapidly across the U.S.

In the 1940s, slot machines were introduced as an amusement for the wives and girlfriends of high-rolling gamblers, but after a few decades they became as popular as table games. By the 1990s the slots surpassed table games in popularity. And, the old mechanical machines used during the 1930s-1960s have all been replaced with modern electronic machines. Today, Las Vegas has more than 200,000 slot machines of every imaginable type.

Slot machines have always been popular because they make few demands on players and have frequent payoffs. These machines, long known as one-arm bandits, have been the gambling industry's most consistent moneymaker. There has never been any other gambling device that has produced such enormous profits with so little effort on the part of the operator.

The Mechanical Slot Machine. A rugged, sturdy, complex device of over 600 parts and many springs, this is the type of machine that were found in Las Vegas casinos during the 1930s-1960s. Put in your coin, pull the handle, watch the reels turn, and hope when they stop you are a winner. Here is a row of slot machines at Circus Circus Casino. Circa 1968, $4-6.

Slot Machines. Some people call them "one-armed bandits," but it was certainly thrilling to hear the merry music of coins jingling out of the machine. Slot machines are one of the first gambling games that a visitor in Las Vegas tries. Many people find it thrilling to drop in a coin, pull the handle, and watch the reels spin... and there's no thrill quite like the shout of "Jackpot." Circa 1950s, $3-5.

Wheel of Fortune. There's never a dull moment on the wheel of fortune! Round and round the wheel turns—who will be the one to pick the lucky winner? Often shouts of players cheer the large carnival-like wheel to stop on their number Circa 1940s, $7-9.

How to Keep Your Shirt When Gambling. The first part of any viable casino strategy is to risk the most money on wagers or events that present the lowest edge for the house. Craps, baccarat and blackjack are the most advantageous to the bettor in this regard. The base line bet at craps, if backed up with full odds, can be as low as .5%. The two types of bets at baccarat have a house advantage of a little more than 1%. Blackjack, at times, can not only put you even with the house (a true 50-50 proposition), but actually give you a slight long-term advantage. How can a Casino possibly provide you with a 50-50 or even a positive expectation at some of its games? The first reason is because a vast number of suckers make the bad bets (those with a house advantage of 5%-35%, such as roulette, wheel of fortune, and slot machines) day in and day out. The second is because they know that very few people are aware of the opportunities to beat the odds. Finally, because it takes skill—and study and practice—to be in a position to exploit these opportunities. However, a mere hour or two spent learning strategies for the beatable games will put a person light years ahead of the vast majority of visitors who give the gambling industry an average 12-15% profit margin. Circa 1950s, $3-5.

Wheel of Fortune

The wheel of fortune (also called the big six wheel) is a carnival like wheel with fifty-six positions on it, fifty-four of them marked by bills from $1 to $20. The other two spots are special symbols; each pays 40 to 1 if the wheel stops in that position. All other stops pay at face value. Those marked with $20 bills pay 20 to 1, the $10 bills pay 10 to 1, and so forth. The idea behind the game is to predict (or just blindly guess) what spot the wheel will stop at and place a bet accordingly. The dealer will spin the wheel and the "number" it stops on is the "number" that wins. It is a simple game to play. The odds on almost any of the many variations of the wheel of fortune are terrible. They aren't meant to be good, and neither are they meant to attract any real gambler. If the "lookers" want to play them, welcome aboard! The large wheel turning slowly around has a magnetic effect on many players.

Chapter Eleven:
Buffets & Restaurants

Every hotel and casino in Las Vegas went overboard to keep gambling patrons in their facilities. Eating was never a problem. There were restaurants, coffee shops, cafes, buffets, lounges, and other eateries. During the 1950s and 1960s the buffets were big attractions—all the food you could eat for $1.50. For little more than pocket change, gambling patrons could eat! eat! eat! and come back for more. The Silver Slipper Gambling Hall offered a 69¢ breakfast. This caught on and every hotel on the Strip started offering a bargain breakfast. The midnight-to-dawn buffet was also popular with patrons after an evening in the casino. Bargain prices occurred in hotel and casino restaurants because they recouped their losses from patrons losing money on the slot machines and gaming tables.

Capitalizing on the Fun. In the 1940s many restaurants, gas stations, drug stores, grocery stores, and other businesses had a few slot machines. Shown is the Swiss Village restaurant located at 116 North Fifth Street in downtown Las Vegas. Circa 1940s, $6-8.

Cattleman's Restaurant. The gourmet restaurant at Bonanza Hotel and Casino was Cattleman's Restaurant. At the door was Maitre'd, Leslie Southern, an Englishman from Yorkshire, who had sailed aboard British passenger ships for twenty years. The first impression you had of the restaurant was that you had entered a railway car. You had! It was an authentic replica of the world famous millionaire Lucius Beebe's Dining Car. To the left was the "Crazy Horse" saloon and, down a few steps, the main area of Cattlemen's, an area for lovers of fine food and atmosphere. Upstairs were the "Bordello" rooms. They were quaint and secluded dining rooms furnished with rare antiques from private collections. Each of the "bordello" rooms were named after a notorious "madam;" on the wall in each of the rooms was a framed history of their lives and exploits. The rooms were named after such famous ladies as Fannie Hill, Sally Stanford, Polly Adler, and Roxie, who had her thriving establishment a few miles from the Bonanza. The FBI raided it and closed it down in 1954. Here is a view of the Lucius Beebe railway car. Circa 1967, $5-7.

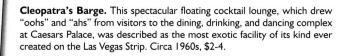

Cleopatra's Barge. This spectacular floating cocktail lounge, which drew "oohs" and "ahs" from visitors to the dining, drinking, and dancing complex at Caesars Palace, was described as the most exotic facility of its kind ever created on the Las Vegas Strip. Circa 1960s, $2-4.

Top of the Dunes Restaurant and Cocktail Lounge. From the Top of the Dunes Restaurant and Cocktail Lounge, 24-stories tall, there was a majestic view of fabulous Las Vegas and the sweeping panorama of the mile-long 18-hole Dunes Championship Emerald Green Golf Course and Country Club (Nevada's largest). The restaurant, enclosed in glass, provided guests with a spectacular view of the 900-square mile Las Vegas Valley. During the evening hours name dance orchestras, such as Freddie Martin and Russ Morgan, played. Circa 1960s, $4-6.

Menu Cover, "Casino de Paris" Dinner Show, Dunes Hotel and Casino. Circa 1960s, $12-14.

"Dome of the Sea." One of the most spectacularly designed gourmet restaurants in Las Vegas was "Dome of the Sea" in Dunes Hotel and Casino. The dining room was sort of seashell-shaped. As visitors sat in a sea of blue-and-green tablecloths and chairs, a steady movement of flying fish was projected slowly around the walls. They created a feeling of being in the midst of the undersea world of King Neptune. Varicolored lights, poured through a domed ceiling, added to the atmosphere. Sitting in a gondola in a nearby pool was a mermaid with long, blond hair playing a harp. The restaurant had a varied gourmet menu of steaks, chops, and chicken, but most items were seafood. Circa 1960s, $5-7.

Menu Cover. Dinner menu cover for the "Casino de Paris" show at Dunes Hotel and Casino. The only place in town where one could get a slice of "Casino de Paris" Cream Pie for 70¢. Circa 1960s, $14-16.

Round-Up Room. At the dinner-supper room in El Rancho Vegas Hotel, there was dancing to big name orchestras. Two floor shows were presented nightly, featuring top talent, with never a cover charge or minimum. Entertaining in the rustic 250-seat dining room (the largest in town) on opening night were Pierre Carta and his Desert Caballeros, singer Lorraine de Wood, dance specialist Dan Hoctor, and Petite Chiquita, dancer from South of the Border. The opulent atmosphere of El Rancho Vegas lured many celebrities to Las Vegas, which was taking its first major step in its climb to international acclaim as the entertainment capital of the world. Circa 1941, $5-7.

El Rancho Vegas Hotel's Restaurant. The sender of this postcard of the El Rancho Vegas Hotel's restaurant wrote: "Having loads of fun here. Caught a couple shows last night—Tony Martin, Dancing Waters, Guy Lombardo and a terrific comedian." Cancelled 1957, $5-7.

Menu Cover, Stage Door Steak House, El Rancho Vegas Hotel and Casino. Circa 1940s, $20-22.

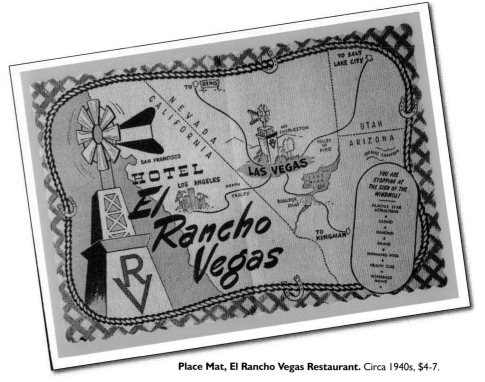

Place Mat, El Rancho Vegas Restaurant. Circa 1940s, $4-7.

Menu Cover, Flamingo Hotel and Casino. Circa 1953, $5-7.

Golden Nugget Gambling Hall Restaurant. Printed on the reverse side of this Golden Nugget Gambling Hall restaurant postcard: "See the old-style west in our modern world. A place of mahogany bars, crystal chandeliers, with the genuine hospitality and old time gaiety of the Barbary Coast and the Virginia City of fifty years ago." Circa 1946, $7-9.

Menu Cover, Golden Nugget Gambling Hall's Restaurant. Circa 1950s, $20-22.

Saloon, Golden Nugget Gambling Hall. A Beals "Art-Tone" salesman's advertising postcard, it was produced in quantities of either 12,500 or 25,000. The price was $4 for 1,000 cards. Circa 1946, $6-8.

Place Mat, Golden Nugget Gambling Hall's Restaurant. Circa 1940s, $5-7.

The Congo Room. Sahara Hotel and Casino presented a new concept in theatrical restaurant arrangement and appearance in their Congo Room. Completely terraced for ringside visibility. Circa 1952, $2-4.

Menu Cover, Silver Slipper Gambling Hall Restaurant. One egg, potatoes & toast, 45¢ ; waffles, 40¢; Rancher's breakfast, 90¢; hamburger, French fries & salad, 49¢; and steak sandwich, French fries & salad, $2. Circa 1950s, $22-24.

Bibliography

Anderson, Frances and John Chase. *Las Vegas: The Success of Excess*. London, England: Ellipsis London Limited, 1997.

Bain, Joseph H. and Eli Dror, Editors. *Casinos: The International Guide*. Port Washington, New York: B.D.I.T. Inc., 1992.

Basten, Fred E. and Charles Phoenix. *Fabulous Las Vegas in the 50s*. Santa Monica, California: Angel City Press, 1999.

Berman, Susan. *Lady Las Vegas: The Inside Story Behind America's Neon Oasis*. New York, New York: TV Books, 1996.

Best, Katharine and Katharine Hillyer. *Las Vegas: Playtown U.S.A.* New York, New York: David McKay company, 1955.

Block, Robert and Mark P. Block. *Las Vegas Lights*. Atglen, Pennsylvania: Schiffer Publishing Ltd, 2002.

Bourie, Steve. *American Casino Guide*. Dania, Florida: Casino Vacations, 2006.

Browne, Rick and James Marshall, Editors. *Planet Vegas*. San Francisco, California: Collins Publishers, 1995.

Bueschel, Richard M. *Lemons, Cherries and Bell-Fruit-Gum: Illustrated History of Automatic Payout Slot Machines*. Denver, Colorado: Royal Bell Books, 1995.

Bulkin, Rena. *Fromer's 96 Las Vegas*. New York, New York: Simon & Schuster, 1996.

Campbell, Tom and Gary Boulanger. *Las Vegas*. Toronto, Canada: Roger Boulton Publishing Services, 1984.

Campiglia, James and Steve Wells. *The Official U.S. Casino Chip Price Guide*. Atglen, Pennsylvania: Schiffer Publishing Ltd., 2005.

Castleman, Deke. *Las Vegas*. Oakland, California: Compass American Guides, 1991.

Christensen, David G. *Slot Machines: A Pictorial Review*. New York, New York: Vestal Press, 1972.

Chung, Su Kim. *Las Vegas Then & Now*. San Diego, California: Thunder Bay Press, 2002.

Coffey, Frank and Joe Layden. *Caesars Palace: The Complete Guide to Gaming*. Santa Monica, California: General Publishing Group, 1997.

Cohen, Phyllis, Editor. *Experience Las Vegas*. Las Vegas, Nevada: Experience Las Vegas, 1999.

Crampton, C. Gregory. *The Complete Las Vegas*. Salt Lake City, Utah: Peregrine Smith, Inc., 1976.

Destination Las Vegas: The Story Behind The Scenery. Las Vegas, Nevada: KC Publications.

Ferrari, Michelle and Stephen Ives. *Las Vegas: An Unconventional History*. New York, New York: Bulfinch Press, 2005.

Fey, Marshall. *Slot Machines*. Las Vegas, Nevada: Nevada Publications, 1983.

Fleming, Allan, Christian Kolberg and Joanne Downey. *Las Vegas Through the Generations*. Las Vegas, Nevada: Las Vegas Review-Journal, 1995.

Geddes, Robert N. *Slot Machines on Parade*. Long Beach, California: Mead Company, 1980.

Geran, Trish. *Beyond The Glimmering Lights: The Pride and Perseverance of African Americans in Las Vegas*. Las Vegas, Nevada: Stephens Press, 2006.

Green, Michael S. *Las Vegas: A Pictorial Collection*. New York, New York: Sterling Publishing Company, 2005.

Greenwood, Robert. *Nevada Post Card Album: Photographic Views of Nevada 1903-1928*. Reno, Nevada: Fred Holabird Americana, 1998.

Hess, Alan. *Viva Las Vegas: After-Hours Architecture*. San Francisco, California: Chronicle Books, 1993.

Highsmith, Carol M. and Ted Landphair. *Las Vegas: A Photographic Tour*. New York, New York: Crescent Books, 2003.

Jones, Will Fulford, Editor. *Time Out Las Vegas*. London, England: Time Out Guides Limited.

Kellock, Katharine A. *Nevada: A Guide to the Silver State*. Portland, Oregon: Binfords & Mort, Publishers, 1940.

Knepp, Donn. *Las Vegas: The Entertainment Capital*. Menlo Park, California: Lane Publishing Company, 1987.

Krammar, Ed and Avery Cardoza. *Las Vegas Guide*. Washington, D. C.: Open Road Publishing, 1994.

Ladwig, Dieter. *Slot Machines*. Secaucus, New Jersey: Chartwell Books, 1992.

Lenzie, Charles A. *Las Vegas: From Trails to Rails*. Las Vegas, Nevada: Nevada Power Company, 1984.

Martin, Don W. and Betty Woo Martin. *Las Vegas: The Best of Glitter City*. Henderson, Nevada: Discover Guides, 2006.

McCracken, Robert D. *Las Vegas: The Great American Playground*. Fort Collins, Colorado: Marion Street Publishing Company, 1996.

Moe, Albert Woods. *Nevada's Golden Age of Gambling*. Reno, Nevada: Puget Sound Books, 2001.

Moehring, Eugene P. *Resort City in the Sunbelt: Las Vegas, 1930-1970*. Reno, Nevada: University of Nevada Press, 1989.

Paher, Stanley W. *Las Vegas: As it began-as it grew*. Las Vegas, Nevada: Nevada Publications, 1971.

Puckett, Ron and Kenneth Davies. *A Brief Look At Historic Las Vegas*. Las Vegas, Nevada: National Historic Publishing.

Puzo, Mario. *Inside Las Vegas*. New York, New York: Grosser & Dunlap Books, 1976.

Rakauskas, Mary. *Frommer's Las Vegas*. New York, New York: Simon & Schuster, 1989.

Ralli, Paul. *Viva Vegas*. Hollywood, California: House Warven Publishers, 1953.

Reid, Ed. *Las Vegas: City Without Clocks*. Englewood Cliffs, New Jersey: Prentice-hall, 1961.

Reid, Ed and Ovid Demaris. *The Green Felt Jungle*. New York, New York: Pocket Books, Inc., 1963.

Rinella, Heidi Knapp. *The Stardust of Yesterday: Reflections on a Las Vegas Legend*. Las Vegas, Nevada: Stephens Press, 2007.

Roske, Ralph J. *Las Vegas: A Desert Paradise*. Tulsa, Oklahoma: Continental Heritage Press, 1986.

Schneir, Leonard. *Gambling Collectibles: A Sure Winner*. Atglen, Pennsylvania: Schiffer Publishing Ltd., 1993.

Schwartz, David G. *Roll The Bones: The History of Gambling*. New York, New York: Gotham Books, 2006.

Sehlinger, Bob. *The Unofficial Guide to Las Vegas*. New York, New York: Prentice-Hall, 1993.

Sheehan, Jack. *Las Vegas Stories*. Houston, Texas: Pioneer Publications, 1992.

Silberstang, Edwin and John Mechigian. *Las Vegas: An Insiders Guide and Gambling Handbook*. Fresno, California: Funtime Enterprises, 1973.

Sonnett, Robert. *Guidebook to Las Vegas*. Los Angeles, California: Ward Richie Press, 1972.

Sonnett, Robert. *Sonnett's Guide to Las Vegas*. Las Vegas, Nevada: Sonnett's Guide, 1969.

Spanier, David. *Welcome to the Pleasuredome: Inside Las Vegas*. Reno, Nevada: University of Nevada Press, 1992.

Steffner, Sandi and Janice O'Neal. *Nevada Casino Playing Card Guide*. Las Vegas, Nevada: Jim Steffner, 2006.

Stratton, David. *Las Vegas*. New York, New York: DK Publishing, 2005.

Stratton, David. *Las Vegas and Beyond*. Berkeley, California: Ulysses Press, 1993.

Taylor, Richard B. *Las Vegas Hacienda Hotel History*. Las Vegas, Nevada: Bee Hive Press, 1990.

Taylor, Richard B. *Moulin Rouge Hotel History*. Las Vegas, Nevada: Bee Hive Press, 1995.

Thomas, Bob. *Liberace*. New York, New York: St. Martin's Press, 1987.

Thompson, William N. *Legalized Gambling*. Santa Barbara, California: ABC-CLIO, 1994.

Venturi, Robert, Denise Scott Brown, and Steven Izenour. *Learning From Vegas*. Cambridge, Massachusetts: The MIT Press, 1991.

Vinson, Barney. *Las Vegas: Behind The Tables*. Grand Rapids, Michigan: Gollehon Press, 1986.

Vinson, Barney. *Las Vegas: Behind The Tables, Part 2*. Grand Rapids, Michigan: Gollehon Press, 1989.

Visalli, Santi. *Las Vegas*. New York, New York: Universe Publishing, 1996.

Weber, Linda, Editor. *Las Vegas Access*. New York, New York: Access Press, 1993.

Woon, Basil. *The Why, How and Where of Gambling In Nevada*. Reno, Nevada: Bonanza Publishing Company, 1953.

Yenne, Bill. *The Illustrated History of Las Vegas*. New Jersey: Chartwell books, 1997.

Index